Br
5/00

SANTA MARIA PUBLIC LIBRARY

3 2113 00442 8424

D0745821

Discarded by
Santa Maria Library

j946

Millar, Heather
    Spain in the Age of Exploration.

Orcutt Br.   AUG 14 2000

DUE
1/17

BRANCH COPY

GAYLORD MG

SPAIN
IN THE AGE OF
EXPLORATION

With special thanks to Kevin Uhalde,
doctoral candidate in the
Department of History, Princeton University,
for his helpful reading of the manuscript.

CULTURES
OF THE PAST

SPAIN
IN THE AGE OF
EXPLORATION

HEATHER MILLAR

BENCHMARK BOOKS

MARSHALL CAVENDISH
NEW YORK

Benchmark Books
Marshall Cavendish Corporation
99 White Plains Road
Tarrytown, New York 10591-9001

© Marshall Cavendish Corporation 1999

All rights reserved. No part of this book may be reproduced in any form without permission from the copyright holders.

Library of Congress Cataloging-in-Publication Data
Millar, Heather, date
    Spain in the age of exploration / by Heather Millar.
        p.   cm.— (Cultures of the past)
    Includes bibliographical references and index.
    Summary: Surveys the important events in the history of Spain from the voyages of Columbus to 1700 and examines the role of the arts and religion during this period.
    ISBN 0-7614-0303-5 (lib. bdg.)
    1. Spain—Civilization—1516–1700—Juvenile literature. 2. Spain—Civilization—711–1516—Juvenile literature. [1. Spain—Civilization—711–1516. 2. Spain—Civilization—1516–1700.] I. Title. II. Series.
DP171.5.M55   1999
946—dc21   97-2090
                                                                                                    CIP
                                                                                                    AC

Printed in Hong Kong

Book design by Carol Matsuyama
Photo research by Rose Corbett Gordon

Front cover: Defense of Cádiz, by Francisco de Zurbarán, 1634
Back cover: Children Eating Grapes and a Melon, by Bartolomé Esteban Murillo (1617–1682)

Photo Credits

Front and back covers: courtesy of Scala/Art Resource, NY; page 6: *Columbus Crossing the Atlantic,* 1927 (print) by Newell Convers Wyeth (1882-1945). Library of Congress, Washington, D.C./Bridgeman Art Library, London/New York; page 9: Esbin-Anderson/The Image Works; pages 10, 16, 25, 29, 31, 38, 39, 40, 44, 57, 58, 62: Scala/Art Resource, NY; pages 11, 46: Instituto Amatller de Arte Hispanico, Barcelona; pages 13, 33, 37: Giraudon/Art Resource, NY; page 14: By permission of The British Library; page 15: *The Conversion of a Moor,* illustrations to Cantiga 46 from 'Cantigas de Santa Maria', (1221-84) vellum. Biblioteca Monasterio de Escorial, Madrid/Index/Bridgeman Art Library, London/New York; page 18: Michel Zabe/Art Resource, NY; pages 19, 21: Erich Lessing/Art Resource, NY; pages 20, 72: Bridgeman/Art Resource; pages 24, 28, 32, 34, 36: Corbis-Bettmann; page 26: *A View of Seville, 16th Century,* by Anonymous. Museo de America, Madrid/Index/ Bridgeman Art Library, London/New York; page 41: The Metropolitan Museum of Art, The Cloisters Collection, 1955. (55.85) Photograph by Malcolm Varon; page 46: R. Alcazar; page 48: The Viesta Collection, Inc.; page 49: The Metropolitan Museum of Art, The Cloisters Collection, 1969. (69.88) Photograph by Malcolm Varon; pages 50, 51: North Wind Pictures; page 52: *Scenographia Fabricae, the Escorial Monastery in Spain* 1662, by J. Blaeu (1598-1673). Royal Geographical Society, London/Bridgeman Art Library, London/New York; page 55: The Granger Collection; page 64: Corbis-Bettman; page 66: L. Mangino/The Image Works; page 67: Reuters/-Bettmann; page 69: Chlaus Lotscher /Peter Arnold Inc.

CONTENTS

CHAPTER ONE

For God, King, and Gold

On August 3, 1492, three creaking wooden ships sailed west toward the unknown from the small Spanish port of Palos. Leading the expedition was Christopher Columbus, a tall, thin Italian seaman and mapmaker. Columbus had on board eighty-eight volunteers. Some, no

doubt, had thoughts of the sea monsters said to dwell ahead in the unexplored Atlantic. But the men were experienced sailors, willing to gamble for a share of the wealth they hoped to find.

Their goal was the glittering cities that lay in China, India, and Japan. By the old land routes to the East, such a journey could take months. But by sailing westward, Columbus proposed, they could reach the land of gold and spices in a few weeks. The plan was considered possible, but the uncharted route was still fraught with peril. Because of the danger, Columbus had had a difficult time getting support for this voyage. The king of Portugal and several other monarchs had sent

Columbus away, saying his plan was too risky. Finally, however, Columbus had convinced the king and queen of Spain to finance his idea.

Once the explorers were off, the daring trip went slowly. The weeks crawled by—first two, then three, then five. As the narrow, high ships called caravels inched west, the Atlantic began to seem endless. Fear arose and the sailors began to grumble. The captains of two of Columbus's ships pleaded to turn back to Spain; the next day so did the men on his own ship.

Just as hope was all but gone, a sailor spotted a green branch with flowers floating on the water. The branch meant land must be near, and the crews' trust in Columbus returned. Then, at about 2:00 A.M. on October 12, 1492, the nearly full moon illuminated a sliver of white on the horizon. "Tierra! Tierra!—Land! Land!"—the lookout cried. At dawn the sailors saw people on the beach, who fled at their approach. Columbus went ashore in a boat rowed by armed men. He declared that the land now belonged to his patrons, the king and queen of Spain. Falling to his knees, he kissed the ground and gave thanks to God for a safe passage across the sea. He named the land San Salvador, meaning "Holy Savior."

The explorers spent two days on San Salvador, an island that is now part of the Bahamas. Soon they met its

Columbus and his small fleet of three ships make their way across the Atlantic.

men and women, and offered them gifts of red caps and colored beads; in return the people gave them parrots and balls of cotton thread. The Spanish marveled at the natives' friendliness and generosity; they called them Indians, believing they had reached the land of India in Asia.

Further travel took Columbus to what are now Cuba and Haiti before he returned to Spain, bringing with him New World crafts and objects, Indians, and some gold. He admitted that he had not found the fabled cities of China and Japan, with their luxurious palaces and rich markets. But he thought they must have been near, and told stories of incredible riches to be found just over the horizon.

Before long the Spanish would realize that Columbus had not found Asia at all. Instead he had stumbled upon continents unknown to most Europeans: the Americas. Their discovery would bring Spain immense amounts of gold, silver, and emeralds—the wealth to fuel an empire. Columbus marked the beginning of an age of exploration and conquest that would last two centuries and would make Spain, for a time, the richest and most powerful nation on earth.

Toward the Age of Exploration

The broad, square Iberian Peninsula, which consists of Spain and Portugal, juts west out of the continent of Europe and nearly touches Africa. The tip of Spain marks the western limit of the Mediterranean Sea. Separated from the rest of Europe to the north by the Pyrenees Mountains, Spain is washed by the cold Atlantic on the north and west and by the warm Mediterranean on the south and east. In between lies a land of dry, rolling plains and hills broken by mountain ranges and five major rivers. The center of the country is a high, broad plateau having limited rainfall, poor soil, cold winters, and hot summers. From ancient times native Iberians preferred the coastal plains, with their milder weather, more fertile soil, and access to the sea. Season to season, herders migrated from the hills to the valleys, or from the plateau to the coast.

The peninsula was the scene of centuries of battle between peoples who wanted to control the land and gain access to its rich resources of gold, lead, iron, and copper. Around 1000 B.C.E.* various tribes began to

*Many systems of dating have been used by different cultures throughout history. This series of books uses B.C.E. (Before Common Era) and C.E. (Common Era) instead of B.C. (Before Christ) and A.D. (Anno Domini) out of respect for the diversity of the world's peoples.

move into the Iberian Peninsula and to shape its history and culture. From the north, tribes of Celts came and warred with the native Iberians in the brown plains and hills. On the Mediterranean coast, traders from the more advanced civilizations of Greece, Phoenicia, and Carthage set up ports at Cádiz, Málaga, and Cartagena.

In 218 B.C.E. armies of the Roman Empire invaded Iberia and gained control of most of the peninsula. It became one of the empire's most valuable provinces as Iberian gold, silver, and copper

The most westerly point of Spain is called Cape Finisterre, from the Latin finis terre, *"end of the land." This rugged seacoast long marked the end of the world known to Europeans.*

9

enriched Roman rulers and Spanish grain helped feed its people. Some peoples of Spain resisted Roman rule, notably the Basques, who lived in the western area of the Pyrenees Mountains. Yet for six centuries the Romans largely dominated. They built aqueducts and amphitheaters, imposed Roman law on the peninsula, and made Latin the common language. To this day Spanish remains basically a Roman, or "romance," language.

In the fifth century C.E. migrations and invasions of northern tribes began to weaken the Roman Empire. Among the tribes that settled in Spain were the Vandals, the Suevi, and the Visigoths, who intermarried with the local people and converted to Christianity. In their era, the Visigothic rulers created the most successful kingdom to follow Rome. Their architecture, law, and literature rivaled that of any culture in Europe. However, the mixture of cultures and the peninsula's mountainous terrain made it difficult for the Visigoths to control all parts of the country equally.

A splendid room in the Alhambra, the famous Moorish palace and fortress built in the thirteenth century in the city of Granada. The art and architecture of the Muslims left a permanent influence on Spanish design.

By the early eighth century Visigothic power had waned, to be replaced by the rule of Muslim leaders from North Africa. During the Middle Ages, these Arab rulers created a society that was a center of economic and cultural splendor. They generally ruled with tolerance, allowing Christians and Jews to worship in their own ways. Muslim palaces had marble pillars, graceful arches, and refreshing fountains. Iberian cities, linked to a greater Muslim empire that stretched through North Africa and the Middle East, prospered. Goods from Muslim Spain—glass, leather, metalwork, and silk—were renowned throughout the world then known to most Europeans. The complex geometric patterns of their art left a permanent impact on Spanish design.

Science, medicine, and philosophy flourished, especially in the Muslim capital of Cordoba. The Arabs introduced paper—first used in the Middle East around 900 B.C.E.—as well as cotton, rice, sugarcane, and the palm tree. They even gave the Spaniards the word to cheer the bullfighter: *olé* (oh-LAY), from the Arabic *wallah* (Wow! What a surprise!).

Muslims from across the Islamic world settled in the region, which they called al-Andalus. Few Muslims—or Moors, as the Christians called them—chose to settle on the barren highlands. In that region, known as Castile, and in a few other northern areas, Christian enclaves grew into strong kingdoms. The great wish of these Christians was to seize control of Spain from the Moors.

For three centuries small Christian kingdoms battled against the Muslim states that dominated the peninsula. Territory was won for Christianity, then lost. Some Christian and Muslim rulers signed treaties, then did not honor them. But ever so slowly, century after century, the Christian kingdoms won more and more land. Bit by bit they pushed the area of Christian control southward. In 1002, with the death of its ruler, al-Andalus broke up into quarreling factions. Taking advantage of those divisions, the Christian kingdom of Castile, supported by the kingdoms of Aragon and Navarre, led the fight to drive out the Moors. By 1248 only one Muslim kingdom remained: Granada, in the south.

The marriage of Ferdinand and Isabella, seen here in a fifteenth-century manuscript illumination, set the stage for the eventual unification of Spain.

Ferdinand and Isabella

In 1469 two of the most powerful and important Christian kingdoms on the Iberian Peninsula were united by marriage. Isabella I, the eighteen-year-old heir to the throne of Castile and León, wed her cousin, Ferdinand II, the seventeen-year-old king of Sicily and heir to the throne of Aragon. In 1474, upon the death of Isabella's brother, they were crowned queen and king of Castile and León; in 1479, on the death of his father, Ferdinand (but not Isabella) added the crowns of Aragon and Sardinia. All of the Iberian Peninsula except Portugal, Granada, and Navarre now recognized the authority of Ferdinand and Isabella. In many ways, however, Spain was still fragmented.

Until the coming of Ferdinand and Isabella, medieval Spain had been a patchwork of multiple rulers and conflicting laws. Large areas in this vast territory recognized only the justice of local lords and the church. What was lawful in one town might be a crime in another. The average person was far more affected by the power of local noblemen and wealthy merchants than that of a distant king or queen. Ferdinand and Isabella knew that Spain could never be strong while it was so divided. They believed that authority should be centralized in the monarchy, so they set out to unify the peninsula under their rule.

Rather than stay in one capital city, they took care to be present wherever they were required in the realm. They managed government, dispensed justice, and made war—in person. They used the power of their personalities, clever political moves—and, if necessary, force—to win respect for royal authority. In this way, they brought order to the entire country and reformed the royal court. They created the beginnings of a modern bureaucracy. Meanwhile they steadily added to their domain, eventually absorbing the neighboring kingdom of Navarre, colonizing the Canary Islands off the northwest coast of Africa, and gaining control of the Italian kingdom of Naples.

Religious Persecution

During their centuries of war with the Muslims, the people of Castile had adopted an intense devotion to Christianity. The Reconquista, or Reconquest, of Muslim territory, which was led by Castile, had become as much a religious crusade as a military campaign. As a Castilian, Isabella was a woman of deep religious convictions.

Isabella was determined to make her state strong internally. Yet her subjects were a disorderly medley of peoples, languages, and creeds. In 1480 she got permission from the Roman Catholic Church to create a special court to convert or eliminate those who did not follow the teachings of Christianity, specifically Muslims and Jews. Isabella hoped this tribunal would insulate Christians from those who did not share their faith. Called the Spanish Inquisition, this body spent the next three-and-a-half

This painting shows a romanticized vision of Columbus's audience with Ferdinand and Isabella after his return to Spain. In reality Columbus exaggerated his exploits in the New World.

centuries seeking out and prosecuting suspected unbelievers. Those found guilty could be handed over to the government for confiscation of property, imprisonment, or execution. Even Jews and Muslims who claimed to have adopted Christianity fell under suspicion.

The reasons for persecution sometimes went beyond religious consideration. In the province of Valencia, for instance, economics fueled the Inquisition. Some were accused only so that their property could be confiscated. In other areas Christian workers accused converted Muslims because they were competitors for jobs. At higher social levels many converted Jews had been successful in finance and administration. Those jealous of this wealth and power often reported converted Jews to the Inquisition.

For those who refused to convert, matters grew even worse. In 1492, Isabella gave Jews four months to become baptized Christians or be expelled from the country. They were permitted to take only what they could carry. Desperate Jews sold houses for a horse; vineyards changed hands for a piece of cloth.

The 1492 expulsion of the Jews from Spain was not the first instance of official Spanish anti-Semitism. In this early-fourteenth-century drawing, Jews take to the road with only a small portion of their belongings.

Spain's Muslims remained, but in the end they fared little better. When the last Muslim kingdom, Granada, was defeated in 1492, the Christian conquerors guaranteed religious freedom to Granada's Muslims. Ten years later, however, Spain's rulers went back on their word and ordered all Muslims to accept baptism or leave the country. The Spanish crown feared that they might be inspired by religious loyalty to help the Muslim Turks or Muslim pirates from North Africa, both of whom were becoming threats to Spanish empire.

The Muslims protested that when their forefathers had ruled the peninsula, they had allowed Christians to practice their faith. Yet Ferdinand and Isabella stood firm in their decision to expel Muslims who would not convert to Christianity. Though figures differ, hundreds of thousands, and perhaps millions, of Muslims left Spain during the sixteenth century. Other European countries condemned the exile of the

A Muslim converts to Christianity in this thirteenth-century illustration. By the early sixteenth century, all Muslims were forced to convert or leave Spain.

Muslims. In Spain people celebrated, saying, "Religious unity is secured and an era of prosperity is certainly about to dawn."

Partly through force, the subjects of Ferdinand and Isabella followed the banner of Christianity. All of the Iberian Peninsula, except Portugal, now belonged to the royal couple. With the discoveries made by Columbus, Spaniards found themselves at the doorstep of world empire.

Dividing the World

The return of Columbus in early 1493 exploded Europeans' old notions of geography. Suddenly there was what the Spanish called "a new world," and quickly they, with the pope, laid claim to it. As the leader of the Catholic Church, the pope was considered the representative of God on earth and thus was believed to hold authority over all lands and peoples.

On a map the pope drew a line running north and south just west of Africa. All non-Christian lands discovered to the west, he decreed, belonged to Spain. Portugal, whose sailors were making their own explorations, received the lands to the east of the line. But Portugal, fearing the decision would prevent it from seeking its own sea route to the Indies, protested and threatened war with Spain. In a treaty signed in 1494 the line was moved farther west, through the then-unknown eastern bulge of South America.

The shift made possible Portugal's claim to what would become Brazil, first visited by Europeans in 1500, a country whose people to this day speak Portuguese. The remaining lands in what is today called Latin America—from Mexico to Chile— would belong to Spain.

Charles V (Carlos I), shown here in a portrait by the Venetian artist Titian, spoke of himself as "God's standard-bearer." His heraldic symbol bore the legend Plus Ultra, *"Always Farther." Not since Charlemagne in the ninth century had a ruler dominated so much of Europe as did Carlos.*

The Empire Established

The sweetest fruits of Spanish exploration were not to be tasted by the monarchs who funded Columbus's voyage to the New World. Isabella died in 1504, and Ferdinand followed twelve years later, in 1516. The benefits of the Spanish Age of Exploration, and the Spanish crown, would fall to their grandson Carlos. From his father, a northern European prince, Carlos had already inherited the Netherlands and part of a collection of domains known as the Holy Roman Empire. From his mother, the daughter of Ferdinand and Isabella, Carlos inherited Spain's domains. Eventually he came to wear the crowns of seventeen kingdoms as Charles V, Holy Roman Emperor.

The Spanish at first resisted the rule of this king, known as Carlos I in Spain. Just seventeen when he arrived in Spain to claim his inheritance, he had grown up in Belgium, part of his father's realm. The Spanish considered him a foreigner. Gradually, though, Charles became Carlos; that is, he became more and more Spanish. He spent much of his time on the Iberian Peninsula, learned to speak Spanish fluently,

© Oxford Cartographers

and adopted many Spanish customs. During his forty years on the throne, he spent sixteen years in Spain, more time than anywhere else in his empire, which embraced most of central Europe, including Germany, Austria, Hungary, Bohemia, and a large part of what is now Italy.

It was the wealth flowing from Spain's new territories that provided an ever-growing share of the empire's finances. As a result, Carlos as emperor appointed more and more Spaniards as generals of his armies abroad, governors and viceroys of his provinces outside of Spain, and advisers in his councils. Spain thus became the first among equals in the *monarquía* (mon-ar-KEY-ah), also known as the Grand Alliance of Seventeen Crowns. Each realm, or crown, had its own government and its own laws; they were united only in their loyalty to Carlos. But as Carlos became more and more identified with Spain, Spaniards began to consider the entire empire Spanish.

As head of the Grand Alliance, Spain was able to draw upon its allies for the tools that would build its empire: the naval expertise and military manpower of Genoa and Naples, the weaponry of Milan, the financial backing of Antwerp bankers. In turn Spain provided its allies with markets, profits, and employment.

In Europe Carlos spent most of his reign defending his empire against three enemies: France, the Muslim Turks, and a new religious movement, the Reformation, which led to a breach between the Catholic Church and reformers whose beliefs and practices came to be called Protestant.

In the Americas Spanish soldiers, or conquistadores, marched forward, first through the Caribbean, then through Mexico and Peru. Though their armies were small, the Spaniards' advanced weapons and horses (new to the Americas) terrified and easily defeated the Native Americans. In 1519 Hernán Cortés landed in Mexico, where he found the great Aztec civilization and its capital city of stone palaces and pyramid temples. The Aztecs thought Cortés was a god and at first accepted his rule. Later war broke out, and Cortés, with the aid of the Aztecs' enemies, succeeded in defeating them. During the 1530s another conquistador, Francisco Pizarro, exploring Peru, came upon the terraced mountain villages and stone cities of the Inca empire. By trickery Pizarro seized the Inca leader, collected an enormous ransom of gold and silver, then executed his captive and began centuries of oppression.

Spanish exploration and conquest, meanwhile, continued in other parts of the world. In the 1520s, during a Spanish-backed trip that made him the first man to sail around the world, Ferdinand Magellan discovered a large group of islands in Asia. In honor of Carlos's son Felipe (feh-LEE-pay), or Philip II, the islands were named the Philippines—the name still used today. In the 1580s Spain annexed Portugal and Portuguese holdings in the Americas, Africa, and the Far East. The empire of Spain was indeed one on which the sun never set.

A European artist's view of the reception of Cortés by the Aztecs. The Aztecs believed the bearded, white-skinned conqueror was a god returning to lay claim to Mexico.

The Victoria, *the ship that took Ferdinand Magellan around the world*

Empire, Faith, and Sea Power

Starting in 1555 Carlos began to give up his duties, leaving the Holy Roman Empire to his son Ferdinand and giving Spain and his other dominions to his son Felipe. Under Felipe Spain was to see both the height of its power and the increasing economic burdens that would eventually leave the nation exhausted.

Felipe was tall, thin, hardworking, and deeply devoted to the Catholic faith. Rather than leave the tasks of government to advisers, he preferred to do things himself. His eyes were often red from reading government documents late into the night. Though he rigidly insisted on obedience to royal rule and the church, he was also concerned for justice, which won him the love of the Spanish people.

But there was little love for Felipe outside of Spain, where a growing number of enemies envied his kingdom's success. Spain seemed unstoppable. Twice a year great fleets of armed merchantmen sailed from Seville to collect wealth from the Americas. The ships returned low in the water, heavy with gold and silver bars (bullion) from the mines of Mexico and Peru. Spain seemed to have found a limitless supply of riches. Such wealth brought immense power. Under Felipe, Spain's wealth paid for an army of 50,000 men noted for their bravery and discipline and for a navy of 140 vessels.

Francis Drake's voyage around the world brought him £600,000 (billions of dollars in modern American money) and gave the queen £275,000. She dined on his ship, made him a knight, and called him "the greatest seaman and pirate of his age."

Today pirates are the stuff of stories and legends. They're no closer to us than the make-believe of Captain Hook in the tale of Peter Pan. But during the Age of Exploration, pirates were very real indeed. English, French, Dutch, Turkish, and North African pirate ships lurked along the Spanish sailing routes. All hoped to steal Spanish cargo. It was a time of cannonballs and sword fights—and even one-legged men with parrots.

The pirate the Spanish most hated was a proud, red-headed Englishman named Francis Drake. At twenty-two Drake found himself on a pirate ship filled with Spanish treasure. The ship was attacked by the Spanish. After numerous adventures, Drake made it back home with nothing more than his reputation for bravery and a determination to avenge himself against Spain. At twenty-five he got a secret pirate, or privateer, commission from the English queen, Elizabeth I. This gave him permission to capture what he could of Spain's treasure. Spain's pirate was England's hero.

At twenty-eight Drake captured a Spanish fleet loaded with silver. He had his revenge. Spain howled for Drake's death. The queen hid Drake for three years. Then she outfitted him with four ships and sent him out to sea again. Drake crossed the Atlantic and turned south. He sailed all the way to the tip of South America. Reaching the Pacific Ocean, he turned north, raiding Spanish vessels and towns along the way. After going as far as San Francisco, Drake pushed across the Pacific, around Asia and Africa, and then home to England. Elizabeth made him a knight. Soon he was back in the Caribbean burning Spanish ports and sinking Spanish ships.

In Spain Sir Francis Drake was almost as feared as the devil, and mothers hushed their children by whispering, "Drake is coming."

Spanish strength played a key role in 1571, when an international Christian navy gathered off the coast of Greece and soundly defeated the Muslim Turkish fleet at the battle of Lepanto. But at almost the same time, Spanish military strength began to be challenged in another part of the empire, the Netherlands.

Aided by support from England, the Spanish provinces now known as the Netherlands declared themselves independent in 1581. Spain's insistence that it alone could trade with its colonies had led to growing tensions between Spain and England. By trying to keep the riches of the Americas to itself, Spain made other nations angry and jealous. England and others outfitted pirate ships to steal what they could not get legally.

These semi-official raiders sank many Spanish treasure ships and attacked Spanish ports in the Americas. Felipe came to believe that the only way to block aid to the Dutch rebels and end the attacks on the bullion shipments was to invade England. The fact that England was Protestant also spurred the devout Felipe.

The End of Empire

Felipe amassed a fleet of 130 ships for the assault, manned by 8,000 sailors and carrying 19,000 soldiers. He called it the Invincible Armada but from the time it was assembled in 1588, it was plagued with problems. Its first commander died. Then additional troops that it was supposed to pick up never arrived. At sea the Spanish ships were outmaneuvered by the smaller English vessels, and the Spaniards' wooden hulls, though three feet thick, were penetrated by English ammunition.

Carried by the wind to the North Sea, the broken remnants of the Armada made their way around the British Isles, battling terrible storms; day after day, vessels sank and dead men dropped

The defeat of the Spanish Armada, shown here in a Dutch painting, marked the end of Spain's dominance of the seas.

into the sea. Of the 130 ships that had left Spain, 54 returned; of 27,000 men, 10,000 survived, most of them sick or wounded. The catastrophe very nearly bankrupted Spain, which would never again be the most powerful nation on the seas.

But the defeat of the Armada was far from being Spain's only problem. The farthest-flung empire on earth had to be closely governed, from the frontier towns of Mexico and Peru, to the European cities of Milan and Antwerp, to the steamy islands of the Philippines. The armies and navies that defended the empire had to be paid, and the goods that supplied it had to be bought or made. Although Spain outwardly remained a major power, the strain was beginning to show.

Meanwhile the influx of precious metal had pushed prices sky high. Gradually Spain allowed its wealth to depend more on the importation of gold than upon native agriculture and industry. As a result, the crown was forced to buy goods from other countries to supply its colonies. It had to

WHAT HAPPENED TO THE INDIANS?

Spain's Age of Exploration was a disaster for the people already living in the New World. Their leaders were overthrown and their temples were taken apart to provide stone for Christian churches. A few brutal soldiers trained their dogs to have a taste for human flesh, then set them loose to attack the natives. Millions became ill and died because they had no defenses against European diseases like smallpox and cholera. Spanish governors forced Indians to abandon their villages to work in gold and silver mines. Grim records survive, telling of mines where one could not walk because of the jumble of Indian bones. No one is sure how many Indians died because the Spanish came to the Americas; estimates range from 25 million to 75 million.

The record of early conquest does not reflect well upon Spain. Not all of the Spanish explorers were evil, although certainly some were. From the beginning, the Spanish monarchs were genuinely concerned that the natives be treated properly. In the early sixteenth century King Ferdinand and Queen Isabella said that the natives would be treated as Spanish subjects if they accepted the pope as the ruler of the world. If they did not, they would lose their liberty and their property. The conquistadores undercut the spirit of the royal order by reading it in Spanish, which the Indians did not understand.

More than anything, Spain wanted the wealth of the Americas. Abuses continued as native peoples worked the gold and silver mines. Justice for the Indians was forgotten in the demand for profits.

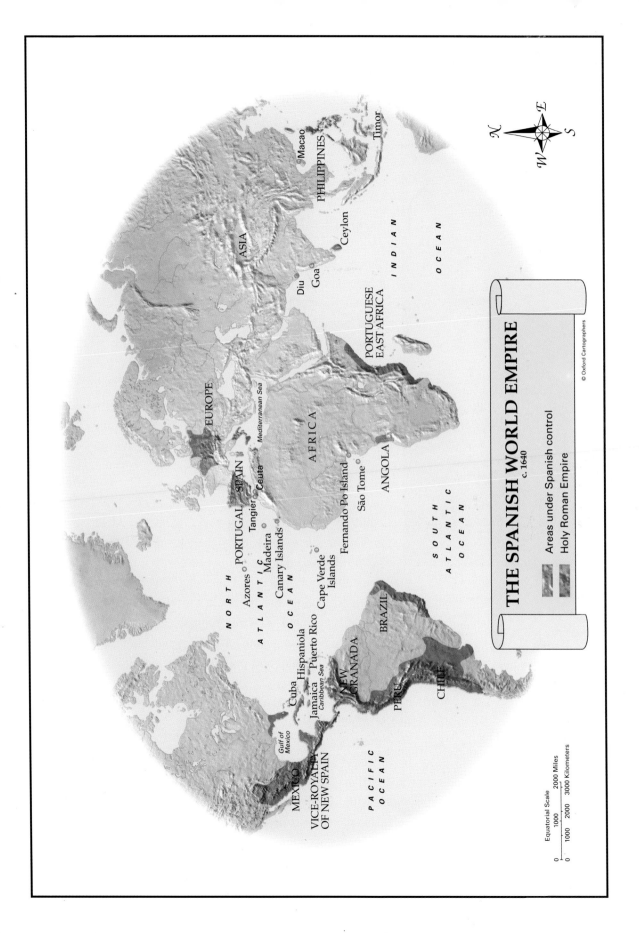

THE SPANISH WORLD EMPIRE

c. 1640

Areas under Spanish control

Holy Roman Empire

© Oxford Cartographers

Equatorial Scale

1000   2000 Miles

1000   2000   3000 Kilometers

0

0

Macao

PHILIPPINES

Timor

ASIA

Ceylon

INDIAN

Goa

OCEAN

Diu

PORTUGUESE
EAST AFRICA

EUROPE

AFRICA

Mediterranean Sea

SPAIN

PORTUGAL

Ceuta

ANGOLA

Tangier

São Tomé

Madeira

Fernando Po Island

Azores

Canary Islands

NORTH

Cape Verde
Islands

ATLANTIC

SOUTH

OCEAN

ATLANTIC

Cuba   Hispaniola

OCEAN

Puerto Rico

Jamaica

Caribbean Sea

NEW
GRANADA

BRAZIL

Gulf of
Mexico

PERU

MEXICO

CHILE

VICE-ROYALTY
OF NEW SPAIN

PACIFIC

OCEAN

Felipe IV, depicted here in a portrait by the court painter Velázquez, was intelligent and well-meaning, but lacked force. He left a dangerously weakened kingdom to his son, the sickly Carlos II.

borrow money to do this and to pay the soldiers that defended its lands. Soon most of the treasure from Mexico and Peru was going not into Spanish hands, but to settle debts with foreign bankers.

With things in such a state, much depended on Felipe III, who came to the throne in 1598. But this Felipe was a timid, weak man. Quite unable to command, Felipe III handed over power to a Spanish nobleman, the duke of Lerma, thus beginning a century in which royal favorites ruled in place of the monarchs. In a politically popular move that later proved disastrous, the duke of Lerma ordered all Muslims who had embraced Christianity to leave Spain. Converted during and after the expulsion of the Muslims from Spain, they were among the nation's most productive farmers and craftspeople. Their departure ruined Spain's industries and its middle class. The empire's economic problems grew worse.

Felipe IV came to the throne in 1621. Under his patronage there was a flourishing of poetry and drama, painting and sculpture as never experienced in Spain before or since. Like his father, he had little time for governing and delegated his powers to a trusted nobleman, the count-duke of Olivares. Olivares drew Spain into endless wars: against the rebels in the Netherlands; against rebels in Portugal; against Dutch and English pirates, who continued to harass Spanish ships and colonies; and against France, Sweden, Denmark, Austria, and parts of Germany in what came to be known as the Thirty Years' War. These disastrous wars further crippled Spain's economy. In 1643 the French army soundly defeated the Spanish at Rocroi, marking the end of Spain's military dominance in Europe.

In 1665 the crown of Spain fell to Felipe's only surviving son, Carlos II, an invalid subject to strange behavior and convulsions. Spain still survived, but its army and navy were broken. It had lost influence in European politics. Its economy was in collapse. Taxes were so high that people didn't bother to work because they would have to give almost all the money they made to the tax collector. Industry slowed to a near stop. The jobless and homeless roamed the streets. People began leaving the peninsula; the population dropped. Cities decayed. Sickly and unable to father children, Carlos bequeathed what remained of his empire to the ruling dynasty of France. His death in 1700 triggered a long and bloody war between many of the major European powers that cost Spain much of its territory and drew to a close its major role in the Age of Exploration.

For two decades of his reign, Felipe IV ceded his political power to his prime minister, the count-duke of Olivares. Olivares attempted to bring much of Europe under Spain's control. In 1643, however, when his behavior became unbalanced, he was forced to resign and was later exiled. This portrait is by Velázquez.

CHAPTER TWO

THE DANCE OF HONOR, THE PRIDE OF ART

The vibrant culture of Spain has its roots in a geography that allowed it to be influenced by many peoples while remaining somewhat insulated from the waves of change that swept the rest of Europe.

The mountain ranges that ripple across the Iberian Peninsula and the seas surrounding it formed natural obstacles to outsiders and afforded protection from attack. This relative isolation nurtured an independence of spirit and national pride, though it also slowed Spanish participation in the culture of greater Europe.

The lure of Spain's natural riches drew to it a variety of peoples of differing cultures and religions—Jewish, Islamic, and Christian—who wove a complex tapestry of artistic expression uniquely Spanish. These diverse forces, both religious and political, encouraged growth of a temperament that was nationalistic and deeply suspicious of foreign ways.

At the height of Spain's Age of Exploration, other European nations struggled with changing views of government, religion, and personal freedom that would ultimately usher in the modern era. The culture of Spain, however, continued to revolve around essentially medieval ideals of religion and honor, social status and nobility. These values influenced not only the way Spaniards lived from day to day, but how they celebrated special occasions, what they chose to memorialize in their art, and what they commented on in their books and in their plays.

Of all the ideals central to the Spanish character during this era, the most important was the "point of honor," the defense of principles that are right, brave, and pure. For "a man who has lost his good name," said one resident of Castile, it is "better for him to be dead than alive." A man who was insulted or accused of wrongdoing would often fight an opponent to the death rather than suffer dishonor.

This concern for upright behavior and reputation reached into all areas of society and had many expressions. Charity, thus encouraged, was widespread. A visitor to a Spanish city of the time would find few beggars among the struggling masses; even in the face of hardship and poverty, Spaniards strove for dignity. Because an honorable person did not complain about difficulties, people struggled to face their problems with patience and a strong spirit. While they loved the luxuries that money could buy, they neither looked down upon the poor nor groveled before the rich. Many dreamed of adventure, grandeur, and romance as the measure of achievement.

Seville at the height of the Age of Exploration, around 1569. A center for shipbuilding, commerce, and art, Seville was the richest and most populous city in Spain. Note the building on the far right; it was the Tower of Gold, Spain's treasury, the place where the wealth of the New World was stored. (artist unknown)

During Spain's heyday the upper classes delighted in showing off expensive clothing. This painting by Zurbarán, Don Diego de Silva, shows a typical court outfit.

In their focus on honor, the Spanish were seeking to live up to a code of behavior that had come down from the noblemen of the Middle Ages. Accordingly almost all Spaniards longed for the prestige of a noble title, and at one point half the nation claimed at least some noble blood. Yet proud heritage did not necessarily mean wealth. The hidalgo—the lowest level of the noble elite, roughly the equivalent of an English knight—was commonly so poor that he became the subject of jokes. For many the only evidence of nobility might be an official paper kept safely in an ironbound box. Though his home might be only a hut, the hidalgo nevertheless made every effort to dress like a king: lace collar, black coat, and buckled boots for a man; veil, fan, and big hoop skirt for a woman. Many hidalgos scorned manual labor, considering it beneath their dignity. In the small towns it was not unusual to see poor nobles who contented themselves with little, slept on straw beds, basked in the sun, strummed their guitars, and avoided the "dishonor" of work.

Those who could not claim even the status of hidalgo might try to achieve special standing in other ways. Some peasants, for instance, claimed "spiritual" nobility. While most nobles had at least traces of Muslim or Jewish heritage from centuries of intermarriage, these peasants would brag that they were "old Christians," descended from the stalwarts of the Reconquista.

Court and Countryside

In Madrid, the city that Felipe II made the capital in 1560, the truly highborn led lives of riches and luxury. On weekdays their usual dress was simple and somber: black suits for men, modest dresses for women. On Sundays and festival days, however, their costumes burst with colorful splendor: starched lace and cloth-of-gold, velvet studded with pearls and gems, and silken puffs and ruffs.

The highest-ranking nobles glided through palace halls hung

with tapestries. Their sitting rooms were decorated with paintings and sculpture by Europe's finest artists. They laughed at the antics of court jesters. They spent their lives attending expensive ceremonies and spectacles: mock battles involving thousands of combatants, religious processions through the city, banquets served on plates of gold.

Among the nobility an air of formality surrounded even the simplest tasks. At the imperial palace, for instance, the king's request for a drink involved an elaborate ceremony: First a servant would fetch a goblet from a nearby cabinet, fill it, and present it to the royal physician for inspection. Then, accompanied by two guards and a footman, the servant would kneel and present the cup to the king. After the monarch drank, the servant would carry the cup back to the cabinet and return with a napkin. Finally the king would wipe his lips. Multiplied in a hundred other ways, such formalities brought everything in the Spanish court—from meals to festivals to official business—to a stately crawl.

Velázquez's portrait of a court jester, Sebastian de Morra, in a somber mood

In the countryside the atmosphere was more relaxed. Still, gracious manners remained the norm even among the peasants in their simple tile-roofed, mud-brick houses. They toiled in groves of olive and orange trees, in vineyards, and in fields of grain. The common people—descendants of Celts, Phoenicians, Carthaginians, Romans, Visigoths, and Moors—carried the weight of the state on their shoulders. Only they, and merchants and traders, paid taxes. The noble classes, including the hidalgos, paid nothing.

Popular Entertainments

In both country and city the toils of daily life were put aside on festival days, which were numerous. There were celebrations for the births and marriages of princes, visits of the king, saints' days, and the dedications of new churches or shrines. In some years holidays outnumbered working days.

Almost all festivals included dancing. As a playwright of the time wrote, "He is not a Spaniard who does not dance as he emerges from his mother's womb." In certain processions professional dancers, male and female, performed dances based on religious stories. People sometimes danced in church. In their palaces the grand people of the court bowed and swirled in formal, organized dances such as the pavane, the branle, and the allemande. In public squares and homes, the common people performed folk dances that could become frenzied while guitars throbbed, tambourines jingled, and hands clapped.

Since a grand and noble appearance was so prized, many Spaniards loved masquerades, parades of people in elaborate dress or in fanciful costumes. Religious festivals and royal celebrations often included a masquerade night. At these fashion events women showed off their newest gowns and ornaments and often covered their faces with mysterious veils. Young men enhanced their best lace collars and cuffs with splashes of perfume. The king and lords of the court rode through the city wearing elaborate outfits of silver and gold cloth. The common people lined the streets to enjoy the splendor.

Man Versus Bull

Spain's most renowned spectacle was the bullfight, which originated on the Mediterranean island of Crete and was brought to the Iberian Peninsula by the Romans. By the Age of Exploration the bullfight had become Spain's national pastime. People would gather around a closed, central square and watch as nobles on horseback thrust spears into a huge, charging bull. After these matadors exhausted the bull, they withdrew from the square. Then the common people would rush forward and slice the unfortunate animal to bits. At once formal and savage, colorful and stately, the ritual of the bullfight embodied the noble virtues of bravery, artistry, and agile intelligence.

During the Age of Exploration, nature was still very frightening: dangerous animals, plagues, floods, and other natural catastrophes menaced people daily. In the bullfight the Spanish could declare at least a temporary triumph by defeating an animal that represented nature in all its power.

During the Age of Exploration bullfights were held in town squares, as shown here in a nineteenth-century painting by Goya.

Still there were some in that day and age who were shocked by the violence of bullfighting. Among them was Pope Pius V, who tried to forbid the sport in 1567. But Felipe II—normally a pious follower of the church—refused to enforce the order. In a letter to the pope, he wrote that the people of Spain would revolt if denied their bullfights.

The Passion for Theater

A close second to bullfights, in the view of the average Spaniard, was the joy to be found in attending plays. Spanish playwrights expressed a sense of honor and a passion for the things of both heaven and earth. Their works combined the noble dreams and the tough realism that ran through the lives of the people.

During the Age of Exploration, theaters were not such formal affairs as they are today. Usually a theater was just a temporary wooden structure thrown up in the main square. A stage occupied one end, and a balcony for women occupied the other. Most male spectators stood in the middle, or "pit." Performances went on daily in Madrid and played to packed houses.

A Spanish theater in the 1600s, built in the open air, in a courtyard

Spain produced what is considered the first modern play, *La Celestina*, written by Fernando de Rojas (1465–1541) sometime after 1492. The play's twenty-one acts made it so long that it was never performed in its entirety; some have said it is not a play at all but a novel written in dialogue. The story concerns two young lovers, Calisto and Melibea, brought together by the Celestina (Celestial One), an old matchmaker. When Calisto is killed in a fall, Melibea commits suicide. The setting of the play is a city, where new concerns for money and passion conflict with traditional values like religious faith and hard work. The play mixes high- and low-style comedy with tragedy and is one of the first works of Spanish literature to portray life realistically.

Most other plays, or *comedias*, dating from the Age of Exploration involved nearly superhuman characters. These larger-than-life figures represented honor in its highest form, love at its purest, evil at its most wicked. They interacted in fantastic plots that revolved around honor, intrigue, and romantic love. Each play consisted of three acts. In between the acts, clowns and other entertainers performed short, funny skits. The characters portrayed in these interludes came from everyday life: hidalgos, beggars, soldiers, pretty women.

The master of the dramatic art form was Lope Félix de Vega Carpio (1562–1635), which for convenience is usually shortened to Lope de Vega (LOH-pay day VAY-guh), or simply Lope. Like many Spanish creative people of his era, Lope lived as an adventurer and romantic before settling down to write. He drew upon the experiences of his adventurous life to create vivid characters for an incredible number of plays: Estimates range from eight hundred to fifteen hundred, of which about five hundred survive. Along the way Lope virtually revolutionized the theater. He

ADVENTURES OF A WRITER

The life of the mind is enough adventure for most artists. But many of Spain's painters, sculptors, and writers lived lives full of real adventure: narrow escapes, mad love affairs, knife and sword fights, dangerous ocean voyages. Consider the life of the playwright and poet Lope de Vega.

Lope was born in Madrid in 1561 of a poor but noble family. At fourteen he ran away from home and school and enlisted in the army. He participated in a few bloody battles in the Azores Islands. He fell in, then out of, love. He wrote some insulting poems about an ex-girlfriend and was sued for damaging her reputation. The courts banished him from Spain, but Lope sneaked back into Madrid. He kidnapped a young girl and married her. The authorities and the girl's male relatives pursued him. To avoid being captured, Lope joined the crew of one of the Armada ships then preparing to invade England.

When his wife died, Lope started an affair with an actress, who was already married with three children. Nevertheless the actress bore Lope two children. Lope left the actress and married an older woman with money. She died, and Lope decided to become a priest. But no sooner had he taken his priestly vows than he started an affair with yet another married woman!

Lope spent his old age in a cottage purchased for him by the government. When he died in 1635, he was almost penniless—and hailed as one of Spain's greatest writers.

rejected the ordered structure of Spanish drama and instead wrote complicated plots that extolled love and defended the monarchy and the Christian faith, while combining both tragic and comic elements. Lope's work paved the way for an entirely new sort of drama, the so-called comedies of cloak and dagger.

One of Spain's greatest writers, Lope de Vega, led a life of high adventure and romance.

Lope's most famous play was *La Estrella de Sevilla* (la ess-TRAY-ah day seh-VEE-ah), or *The Star of Seville*. In this play, as in nearly all his others, the plot turns upon two things: first, a point of honor—in this case proving one's innocence after being accused of a crime—then, who gets the girl. The public never tired of variations on these themes.

The success of Lope's formula inspired many imitators, among the most important of whom was Tirso de Molina (1584–1648). He composed *The Trickster of Seville*, which introduced Don Juan, an unscrupulous and obsessive pursuer of women who is eventually damned for his immorality. The character has haunted the European imagination ever since, in numerous works of music, literature, and art.

Universities and the World of Letters

The energy of the Age of Exploration invigorated Spanish literature. Heroic subjects, soaring emotion, intense patriotism, a mixture of hope and realism—all found their place in the poems, histories, essays, and novels of the sixteenth and seventeenth centuries. Poets like Garcilaso (gahr-sih-LAH-soh) de la Vega (1501–1536) created worlds of imagination that glorified love and beauty. Others sang the praises of the Christian faith and of Spanish military victories. As Spain's fortunes rose, some added to the national glory by writing histories. Yet others, such as Francisco Gomez de Quevedo y Villegas (1580–1645), mocked the self-congratulation of the time. Quevedo (kay-VAY-doh) penned plays, as well as poems and essays, criticizing kings, officials, and popes. Others wrote about *pícaros*, or "rascals," in what are called picaresque novels that concerned bandits, impossibly gallant soldiers, or country love affairs.

With so much activity, the world of letters captured the public imagination. Many educated people went to literary debates with the excitement that people today reserve for sports matches. Writing became a general activity in which large numbers took part. This was particularly true of poetry; almost everyone with some education—artisans, students, and nobles alike—tried his or her hand at rhyme.

Much of this activity went on in the universities. Then, as today, many college students had to content themselves with the simplest of meals and the cheapest of living arrangements. Hunger was familiar in university life. Still, if he could afford it, every young student yearned to hear the lectures of famous men. Two schools towered above all others: Salamanca and Alcala. Salamanca, Spain's first university, cultivated a democratic spirit and embraced new disciplines, such as the study of law. Alcala was more conservative and concentrated on traditional subjects

The doctor of law shown in this painting by Zurbarán taught at the University of Salamanca. Salamanca had seven thousand students in 1584. Its rival school, at Alcala, had only two thousand enrolled.

such as religion and the literature of ancient Greece and Rome. The two schools were, and remain today, the Harvard and Yale of Spain.

In addition to these celebrated schools, hundreds of new academies opened during the mid–sixteenth century; the growing empire demanded it. The government needed new officials to draft regulations, scribes to write them out, and other officials to make sure the rules were enforced. Trade had to be monitored. Financial records had to be kept. Business people and commoners had to be taxed. All of these jobs required educated workers.

Spain's Most Famous Story

Strangely, no one knows whether Spain's best-known author went to college or not. What is known is that Miguel de Cervantes Saavedra (1547–1616) was arrested for dueling and was banished from Spain for ten years. He took part in Spain's great naval victory over the Turks at Lepanto and was wounded in battle, losing the use of his left hand. Not long after Lepanto, Cervantes was captured by pirates and held prisoner. His sisters gave up their wedding dowries and his mother worked for five years to raise the money for his ransom. Returning to Spain penniless and with but one good hand, Cervantes started writing to make a living.

In 1605 a novel by Cervantes appeared in Madrid. The book, *Don Quixote de la Mancha* (don kee-HO-tay day lah MAHN-chah), was about the adventures of a gentleman named Don Quixote. (Don is a Spanish title of honor.) The lean old man reads too many romances and comes to believe that he is a knight, destined to fight giants and rescue damsels in a return to medieval chivalry. The story of the idealistic don and his companion, Sancho Panza, struck a chord in the hearts of the Spanish people, who rushed to buy it. It continues to be widely read today and is the source of many popular sayings, including "Honesty's the best policy," "I'll turn over a new leaf," and "Thank you for nothing."

Paintbrush and Canvas

A lasting gift of the Age of Exploration was the flowering of Spanish art, particularly painting, still celebrated today in museums around the world. Intense, expressive works were commissioned to decorate and enrich churches and cathedrals across the land. After the church, the Spanish court and nobility were the strongest patrons of art, especially favoring

THE MAN OF LA MANCHA

Spain's great novel, *Don Quixote de la Mancha*, concerns an old country noble, Don Quixote, from a village called La Mancha. The don has spent most of his life in his library, reading tales of gallant knights, fainting damsels, and heroic deeds. Everything the don reads, he believes. Inspired by his books, the tall, gaunt gentleman dresses himself in armor and sets off to defend the oppressed, to right wrongs, to protect maidens and innocents.

The real world turns out to be very different from the world of stories. Don Quixote doesn't let that discourage him. In his mind, the swaybacked horse he rides becomes the gallant stallion Rozinante. The lady to whom he dedicates his mission, Dulcinea, changes from a loud, garlicky peasant girl into a royal princess. The don's fat companion, Sancho Panza, is not a peasant with dirt under his fingernails, but a noble squire.

Together Don Quixote and Sancho Panza have numerous adventures. At one point the don attacks a windmill with his lance, thinking it is a giant monster. The don is thrown into the air and lands on his head. He believes this to be the work of the giants, not a result of his own foolishness.

Through inns and windmills, filthy ditches and stampeding pigs, the don remains the soul of politeness and compassion. Sancho knows that the whole effort is ridiculous, but he stays because he loves the don and admires his faith. At last Don Quixote goes back to his village and regains his reason—but for him harsh reality is madness. Sad and defeated, he dies.

Wounded in war, Cervantes started writing because he had no other way to make a living. He later worked as a public servant, but his political career was as marked by misfortune as his military career had been. Only late in life did Cervantes have enough money to devote his full time to writing.

pieces that celebrated religious themes. Felipe IV spent a fortune on paintings, sending agents to scour Europe for masterpieces. At home he supported Spain's greatest artists, allowing them to expand beyond religious subjects and to begin painting portraits and scenes of everyday life.

The high tide of artistic achievement, known as the Golden Century, began with the arrival in Toledo of Doménikos Theotokópoulos (1541–1614), known to history as El Greco, "The Greek." Among his most famous pictures is *The Burial of Count Orgaz,* showing saints descending to accompany the count to heaven. Each face is as detailed as a finished portrait. The robes dazzle with hues of gold, green, and white. El Greco gradually moved away from the natural style that he had learned while studying in Italy. In his mature years he experimented with an eerie, unearthly light; harsh colors like acid green and brilliant blue; and elongated, distorted bodies that seem to reach for heaven.

Francisco de Zurbarán (1598–1664), Spain's next great artist, painted pictures that seemed realistic but often had a spiritual theme: Christ and his

In 1580 Felipe II asked El Greco to do a painting for him, but rejected it when it was completed. El Greco then started his most famous picture, The Burial of Count Orgaz, *shown here. After this painting was finished, El Greco never lacked for work or praise.*

Velázquez was famous for his portraits of court figures such as the young girl here, the Infanta (Princess) Margarita Teresa. Court ladies wore wicker undergarments called panniers to make their skirts very wide.

mother, apostles and prophets, saints holding symbols of their miracles or sufferings. Santa Lucia (Saint Lucy), for instance, carries her eyes on a platter. Zurbarán dressed his holy subjects in silks, brocades, and flowing capes. His colors were vivid: rose and pale green, orange and deep yellow. With solid sincerity and the power of color and form, the artist spent his life decorating the walls of palaces and churches, convents and monasteries.

Diego Rodríguez de Silva y Velázquez (1599–1660), considered Spain's greatest artist, qualified as a master painter at the age of eighteen. On a visit to Madrid he executed a portrait so perfectly that it attracted the attention of Felipe IV. Seeing it, the king declared that from then on only Velázquez would paint the royal family. Molding bold color and light, he painted endless portraits of overdressed, severe courtiers; princesses being fussed over by ladies-in-waiting; kings with quiet nobility; nobles riding prancing stallions. Between his official projects, he also managed to paint realistic portraits of common people: peasants, cardplayers, worn-out writers, tavern scenes. To all of these pictures, Velázquez brought a deep sense of dignity and realism.

Bartolomé Esteban Murillo (1617–1682) closed the great century of Spanish artists. He was not as original as the others, but he was modest, gentle, pious, and beloved. He painted tender visions of Christian stories and more than thirty different portraits of the Virgin and Child. He loved to paint children, and if he could not fit them into his religious paintings, he painted them independently. In one project he filled a wall with images of children: boys throwing dice, boys eating melon, a boy eating bread while his mother grooms him.

Taken together, the masterpieces of the Age of Exploration combine a distinctly Spanish expressiveness with the realities of empire and the aspirations of religious faith. These achievements continue to influence the world of art.

Murillo was known for his pictures of children. This one is entitled Children Eating Grapes and a Melon.

CHAPTER THREE

THE GLORY OF GOD

The main altar at the cathedral of Santiago de Compostela is lavishly adorned.

In Spain during the Age of Exploration, Christianity influenced all aspects of life. In the northern city of Léon, in Madrid, the capital, in southern Cádiz, and in all points in between, religion filled the lives of the people. Monks wandered the roads in coarse robes and sandals, preaching and hearing the confessions of the faithful. Ordinary people went to church frequently, even daily. They prayed at home several times a day. Sometimes they fasted from food. Everyone, including the poor, gave money to help build the massive cathedrals that punctuated the landscape. Kings and commoners alike loaded the church with gifts. Every event—whether a solar eclipse or a war or a good harvest—was interpreted in religious terms. If a family could afford a book, a very expensive item in those days, it was usually a Bible or a collection of stories about the lives of the saints.

Religion was the foundation of Spanish society. Yet as the Age of Exploration dawned, this foundation showed cracks—differences in belief and creed. As it built an empire, Spain painfully, sometimes brutally, covered these cracks, creating a unity of belief and practice that came to define Spanish Christianity.

Christian Beliefs

In the end, the Christian creed came to dominate the Iberian Peninsula. Since Christianity is still the most common religion in Europe and the Americas, the outlines of the Christian story are familiar even to most non-Christians:

Christians are followers of Jesus, who was a Jew. He was later given the title Christ, which means "Messiah" or "Chosen One"—the one who would deliver humankind from its sins. Christians believe that he was born in Bethlehem to Mary, a virgin, through the power of the Holy Spirit of God. He was reared in the Jewish tradition by Mary and her husband, Joseph.

Jesus grew up to be a carpenter and a preacher. He taught the word of the Jewish

Works of art adorned the walls of Spanish churches. This sculpture, set against a painted landscape, was completed around 1480. Called The Lamentation, *it shows the Virgin Mary and others mourning Jesus afer his death on the cross.*

God, while emphasizing the power of divine love and forgiveness. He offered people—those who believed in him and followed his commandments—the promise of eternal life. According to Christian tradition, Jesus healed the sick and performed many miracles. This gentle man's actions and his philosophy of a loving God soon attracted many followers.

Jesus was not afraid to criticize the people in power, and he began to make them angry by claiming to be the Messiah and by not observing all Jewish laws. Eventually one of Jesus' followers betrayed him and delivered him to the authorities. Jesus was condemned by his fellow Jews as a false Messiah. They turned him over to the Romans who, using a punishment common in those days, crucified him.

Three days later, Christians believe, Jesus rose from his tomb. He urged his followers to go out and teach the message of brotherly love that he had taught. Someday, Jesus promised, he would come again. On that day, the Last Judgment, all souls would be judged, and good would finally triumph over evil.

The Church

In Spain from the fifteenth to the seventeenth centuries there was only one official faith, that of the Spanish Catholic Church. From town to town and from region to region, religious traditions varied. Some believers were mystics, others severely earthbound. In universities scholars raised religious questions. But all believed they were upholding the pillar of their society: the Spanish Church. The church provided the nation's religious ideal. It set the standards of behavior and belief for nearly everyone. The good, it taught, would after death go to heaven, a place of everlasting joy, peace, and beauty. The wicked would be condemned to eternal punishment in hell.

The Holy Battle

It would be hard to overstate how terrifying the prospect of hell was to the average Spanish Catholic. Hell was an underworld of heat and fire, an agony that would never end. In that day and age, Christ was not gentle Jesus, meek and mild. Instead, he was the all-powerful being who punished sin: every bad thought, every wrongful deed, every missed church service.

This interpretation seems harsh today, but during the Middle Ages, the emphasis on the terrors of hell and the promise of heaven helped maintain order. Life remained full of peril in the fifteenth, sixteenth, and seventeenth centuries. Few people died of old age; they were more likely to be carried off young by disaster or disease. Women commonly died in childbirth. Most children did not live to grow up. A man in his forties was considered old. The state laid heavy taxes on the people, and the church, too, expected them to give a percentage of their earnings.

In the midst of daily sadness, the teachings of the Catholic Church gave meaning to life, to loss, to hardship, to poverty.

During the sixteenth and seventeenth centuries, the devil was a living reality to most Spaniards. Many supposed that volcanoes were the mouths of hell. Satan, people believed, prowled everywhere. He disturbed people in their sleep. He and his demons put mean words into people's mouths, cut holes in their cloaks, threw dirt at passersby. Even worse, Satan led people to commit serious crimes like murder and robbery.

In Spain people believed in many demons. Satan reigned at the summit of evil. An army of lesser demons helped him: Lucifer and Beelzebub, then Asmodaeus, the prince of lust; Leviathan, the demon of pride; Belial, the supposed patron of Gypsies, fortune-tellers, and witches; and many others.

People believed that Satan could invade people's souls and "possess" them. People explained all mental diseases as cases of possession. Many signs were thought to indicate possession by the devil: the ability to speak in a language that one had never learned before, swearing in front of holy objects, refusing to pray or to make the sign of the cross.

While some fell victim to Satan, others sought to benefit from his power. Self-proclaimed wizards and witches offered to heal wounds and cure diseases by pronouncing magic words. Witches made love potions and cast spells. Desperate people, it was said, would sell their souls to the devil in return for something they wanted.

People believed that many of these evils could be combated with a splash of holy water or the sign of the cross. Yet even after the devil went away, people said, he left an awful odor like sulfur.

Prayers and Sacraments

Good behavior alone wasn't enough to assure entrance to heaven. One also had to have faith. A person had to believe in Jesus and to rely upon God's grace. The believer expressed that faith through prayer and confirmed that faith by participating in sacred ceremonies.

Prayer—that intimate conversation between believers and their God—was a constant part of Spanish life. Whether kings or peasants, priests or merchants, all Christians were expected to say prayers every day. They prayed after waking, before eating, before sleep. People said prayers if they saw something evil. They prayed if their children were sick or if their house needed a new roof. They prayed in gratitude for good luck or a good harvest or a new baby.

Each major event in a Catholic person's life was marked by a religious ceremony known as a sacrament. By the Age of Exploration the sacraments had been fixed at seven: baptism, confirmation, penance, Communion, marriage, holy orders (becoming a priest), extreme unction (a deathbed rite).

The Virgin appears to a community of monks in this fifteenth-century painting by Pedro Berruguete. Off to the right, one brother does battle with the devil.

The beginning of a Catholic life was marked shortly after birth with the most vital sacrament: baptism. At this ceremony a priest poured water over the head of a baby, symbolically washing away the stain of "original sin"—that is, the sin of Adam and Eve that all people inherited. The baby was touched, or anointed, with specially blessed oil to signify his or her entrance into life with Christ. Those who converted to Christianity as older people also began their new life by being baptized.

At around age seven or eight the Spanish child would receive the second sacrament, confirmation. This rite of anointing with oil, performed by a bishop, confirmed, or completed, the anointing received at baptism. It strengthened and prepared the child to enter into the full spiritual life of a Christian.

The church instilled a great fear of sin and punishment. The sacrament of penance gave people a way to be forgiven for their sins. Christ forgave sins, and he gave that power to his apostles and their successors. To receive the sacrament of penance, a Catholic privately confessed her or his sins to a priest and received absolution, a special prayer and blessing to show God's forgiveness. The priest then gave the person a penance, usually several prayers to be said as a sign of sorrow for sin. Really faithful Catholics put themselves through extra penances, such as going without food for a day or more, or wearing garments of scratchy cloth.

The central sacrament was the Eucharist, or Communion. The church took literally Jesus' words: of the bread, "This is my body"; and of the wine, "This is my blood." Catholics believed that during the Mass, a reenactment of the Last Supper Jesus had with his disciples, Jesus became present in the wine and the bread that the worshippers shared. All Catholics were expected to receive Communion at least once a year.

Marriage was the next sacrament for most Catholics. By making this union holy, the church immensely increased the permanence of the wedding bond. In Spain almost no one got divorced. The ceremony also underscored the duty of couples to have children and to rear them as Catholics.

The last sacrament of a Catholic's life was extreme unction, the special blessing and anointing for a dying person, who might also receive penance and Communion.

The Mother of Jesus

During the Middle Ages the church's stern religious message helped keep order. Over time, however, devotion to Jesus' mother, the Virgin Mary, began to soften that message. By the Age of Exploration, Catholics throughout Europe had started to see Mary as the symbol of motherhood

and of all that was good and gentle and merciful. Mary was said to have been raised bodily to heaven when she died. People believed she could intercede for them with her son. Songs and poems were dedicated to Mary. In cathedrals stained-glass windows, paintings, and statues celebrated her grace and devotion. Knights pledged their lives to her. Mothers prayed to her. Even soldiers and rough tradespeople laid their gifts at places of worship called shrines.

Spanish Catholics were especially devoted to Mary. Many towns raised towering cathedrals to her. People believed that she appeared in different forms at different places. The devout made long journeys, or pilgrimages, to shrines. There were dozens of them, dedicated to Mary, under various titles, such as the Virgin of Pilar in Zaragoza; the Virgin of Guadalupe in the mountains of Estremadura; and the Virgin of Montserrat in the mountains of Catalonia.

The Saints

If Mary reigned above Spanish Catholicism like a mother, the saints were the friends and helpers of the Spaniard. Saints were ordinary people whom the church declared had led especially holy lives. Some saints were martyrs—that is, they gave their lives for their faith. A person could officially be declared a saint only if miracles—amazing deeds, usually cures, that could not be explained by coincidence or reason—were attributed to him or her.

Every nation, city, abbey, cathedral, craft, and problem was associated with a particular saint, called its patron saint. Those who sold perfume prayed to Saint Mary Magdalene. Saint Gall protected chickens; Saint Anthony looked out for pigs. England's patron was Saint George; France's Saint Denis. Spain's patron saint was Saint James the Apostle.

Santiago

James, one of the original followers of Jesus, set out from the Holy Land to teach the world the Christian message. According to legend, James's boat got caught in a storm and ended up in Spain, where he stayed to

At left: Spanish Catholics believed that Mary appeared in many forms and places. In this painting the Virgin of the Navigators spreads a protective cloak over Christopher Columbus and his officers.

SHRINES AND PILGRIMS

In Catholic Spain many places came to be regarded as sacred. These holy spots might be where a vision of the Virgin Mary had been seen or where a miraculous cure had occurred. People also treasured relics—that is, bones or strands of hair from a saint or anything a saint may have used. A relic might be a shoe that a saint had worn or his dinner spoon. Felipe II collected teeth that were supposedly those of Saint Apollonia, the saint invoked against toothache. When he died, Felipe had more than two hundred of these teeth! Christians traveled far and wide to visit relics and sacred sites. These travelers were known as pilgrims and their trips were called pilgrimages. Spain had many sites sacred to pilgrims. Here are a few:

• A cathedral dedicated to Santiago de Compostela became one of the greatest goals of Europe's faithful because it was believed to be the resting place of one of Jesus' first followers, James. Pilgrims to Compostela carried

The statue of the Virgin of Guadalupe

staffs and wore long, hooded cloaks and wide hats that had three scallop shells sewn to them. The shells were symbols of the saint. The Spanish called the stars of the Milky Way "the road to Compostela."

• The shrine to the Virgin of Guadalupe, in the province of Estremadura, dated from the thirteenth century, when Mary appeared to a shepherd who was examining a cow he thought was dead. The shepherd went to get a priest. When he returned, the cow had come back to life. A blackened statue of Mary holding Christ was unearthed from the place where the cow had lain. People enshrined the statue at a nearby monastery.

• In Zaragoza a cathedral housed a sacred pillar and image of the Virgin Mary. Extravagant clothes covered the statue. Priests changed these garments daily.

preach. Seven years later he returned to Jerusalem and was killed by the Roman governor. Tradition holds that James's followers brought his body back to Spain, where he was buried. Over the centuries the location of his grave was forgotten. In Spain Saint James was known as Santiago (sahn-tee-AH-go).

According to legend, in 843, during a battle between Christians and Muslims, a knight mysteriously appeared. He killed all the Moors and then vanished. Christian soldiers said the knight was Saint James. From that moment Spanish Catholics took James as the patron saint of their war against the Muslims. Christians rushed into battle shouting his name.

By the thirteenth century the faithful had built a cathedral at Compostela to honor the saint and shelter what were said to be his remains. Millions of pilgrims from all over Europe journeyed to Santiago de Compostela. Saint James became central to Spain's identity.

Saint Teresa of Avila

During the Age of Exploration, a woman was born who came to be nearly as important to Spain as Santiago. Teresa de Cepeda y Ahumada came from a knightly family of Avila. As her sixteenth birthday approached, Teresa fell ill and almost died. The experience with what is now thought to have been some form of epilepsy touched her deeply and made her think about serious issues like life and death, faith and sin. When she had fully recovered, Teresa decided to become a nun.

In 1535 Teresa entered a convent of Carmelite nuns in Avila. This community, like other Carmelite groups of the time, had veered away from the strict observance of the original Carmelite way of life. Teresa felt called to a more simple, prayerful, and more cloistered, or isolated, form of Carmelite life.

After twenty years in the convent, Teresa experienced a kind of conversion that led her to a closer relationship with God. She saw strange things: burning angels, darts of gold that pierced her heart, balls of light that spoke to her. These visions continued for sixteen years. Her book, *The Interior Castle*, describes her visions and spiritual experiences.

At the age of forty-seven Teresa started a new community.

A fifteenth-century statue of Santiago, Saint James the Great, shows him grasping a staff with a gourd attached. Pilgrims to Santiago's shrine at Compostela carried similar staffs.

The nuns of this first "reformed" convent were called the Discalced (dis-KALST), or shoeless, Carmelites. Teresa believed in simplicity and hard work. "You will find God among the soup kettles," she said. Teresa's Carmelite nuns lived a life of strict isolation, poverty, and prayer. Teresa founded fourteen convents and became Spain's second patron saint.

Saint Teresa of Avila reformed the Carmelite order of Catholic nuns. She insisted on a regimen of absolute poverty, frugal eating, and frequent fasting. Her nuns never wore shoes.

The Jesuits

Meanwhile two more religious leaders were rising in Spain. They would reform the church and move the world.

Don Iñigo de Oñez y Loyola, now known as Saint Ignatius Loyola, was born in a castle in 1491. His wealthy, noble family wanted him to be a soldier. Throughout his childhood Loyola trained to be a fighting man. During his first battle a cannonball broke his leg. Doctors tried to set the bone, but they didn't do it right and had to rebreak it three times. The leg took a long time to heal. During that time, boredom forced Loyola to read and reread the only two books in the castle: one on the life of Christ and another on the lives of the saints. Eventually he got better, but his injured leg was shorter than the other. Thus crippled, Loyola could never hope to fight again. But the books he had read in his sickbed gave him an idea:

perhaps traditional war wasn't so important. Building on the fierce religious tradition of the Reconquista, Loyola became obsessed with another fight: the holy war against those who did not believe in Christianity.

Inspired by this thought, Loyola left his family's castle and its wealth. He gave away his rich clothes and wandered the country in a pilgrim's tunic, studying and teaching. He went to Salamanca and Alcala. He even tried to go to Jerusalem to preach Christianity to the Turks who ruled there.

After several years Loyola ended up in Paris. In that French capital he met another Spaniard: Francisco Javier, who became Saint Francis Xavier. Xavier was handsome, rich, and proud. He enjoyed the good things of life. Gradually Loyola pulled Xavier away from those pleasures of the world and toward spiritual things.

In order to purify themselves and focus their minds on God, the two men started to do spiritual exercises, or penances, together. They whipped themselves. They stood barefoot and almost naked in the snow. They were so dedicated that they inspired others. Soon other men joined their group. The pope ordained Loyola and Xavier priests.

Saint Ignatius Loyola

After a while their group became known as the Compañia de Jesu, or Society of Jesus. People called them the Jesuits. They accepted military discipline. They enlisted for life in a war to spread the Gospel of Jesus Christ. In the centuries to follow, Jesuits became educators, diplomats, and scholars. They took the Christian message to such faraway places as India, China, Japan, and Africa. They became the friends of kings. They started hundreds of schools and universities. Through the Jesuits, part of Spain's mysterious and enthusiastic vision of Christianity reached around the globe.

CHAPTER FOUR

THE CHURCH IN ALL THINGS

E ach massive Spanish church that soared heavenward offered the
promise of salvation. The spiritual influence of the Catholic Church
was all-embracing. It gave people help, guidance, a sense of purpose, even
entertainment. Every town chapel and city cathedral sponsored religious
processions and festivals that relieved the boredom of everyday work.
Almost every week great religious ceremonies and processions filled the

main streets of Spanish towns. During the week before Easter, known as Holy Week, such observances continued almost nonstop.

In addition to its religious authority, Spain's Catholic Church was also a working, human organization that reached into every nook and cranny of the Spanish empire. The church held very real earthly power and controlled vast lands, unimaginable wealth, and great communities of monks and nuns. Believers enriched the church by donating money for buildings, land, and precious objects. Religious officials—priests, bishops and cardinals—became trusted advisers to kings. The church struck fear into the people's hearts as it punished those who questioned its teachings. Religious beliefs gave Spanish conquistadores and sea captains the strength to face impossible odds and build an empire. Faith prodded missionaries to carry the Christian message around the world. It inspired painters and sculptors and playwrights to create great works of art.

Excesses within the Church

However, the Spanish people and the Spanish Church were by no means perfect. A few priests had wives or girlfriends, even though church rules prohibited it. Though monks and nuns were supposed to live lives of poverty, chastity, and obedience, some religious communities ignored these standards. In quite a few monasteries and convents, monks and nuns entertained visitors of the opposite sex, wore expensive clothes, and enjoyed parties and plays.

Despite these occasional excesses, the Spanish people remained enthusiastically devoted to the church. The number of priests and nuns and monks grew steadily during the Age of Exploration. In part this was because Spain's economic problems made desirable jobs scarce. The church offered a lifetime of steady employment and regular meals. For practical as

Above the mountain village of El Escorial, a great monastery-palace dominates the landscape. Built like a fortress, it contains four thousand rooms. It reflects the power of both church and state in Age-of-Exploration Spain.

well as religious reasons, most parents gave at least one son and one daughter to the church. Accordingly, monasteries grew almost as big as towns themselves. By the early seventeenth century more than 32,000 monks lived in more than 9,000 Spanish monasteries.

Spain's Rejection of the Reformation

During the Age of Exploration, Europeans outside Spain began to question Catholic teachings and practices and to condemn the flaws and corruption of some church officials. In 1517 a German priest named Martin Luther nailed a list of ninety-five criticisms to the door of the local church. Luther's list attacked church wealth and corruption. This protester argued that the church must be reformed. Instead of following church doctrine, Luther said, Christians should follow the Bible alone as a rule of faith. He emphasized that individuals could have a direct relationship with God and not depend on priests as intermediaries.

In Germany, in England, in France, in Italy, and in many other European countries, Luther's propositions unleashed a storm of controversy. When the pope banned Luther from the Catholic Church, the former priest set up new churches that abandoned many traditional practices, such as confession. Luther's churches allowed priests to marry and disbanded convents and monasteries. Other religious protesters followed Luther's advice and set up new churches. As a group, these non-Catholic Christian churches came to be called Protestant. This effort to reform the church, called the Reformation, threatened Europe's power structure. With their deepest beliefs at stake, people began to war over differences of religious opinion.

In this battle for the soul of Europe, the Spanish king and people stood squarely on the side of the traditional Catholic Church. Spaniards had spent seven hundred years fighting Muslim rule, slowly winning back their country for Christianity. Only with the coming of Ferdinand and Isabella had they tasted victory in that war. Now they were reluctant to change something for which they had long fought and died.

The Only Faith

By expelling unbaptized Jews and Muslims, Spain had already taken drastic action in the name of religious unity. Of the once populous communities of Jews and Moors, only a fraction remained in Spain. These had accepted baptism rather than brave the terrors of being abused and sent from their homes. Changing religion didn't completely protect the converted Jews, called Marranos, or "swine," nor the converted Muslims, called Moriscos. Many of these converts, also known as *conversos,* became powerful in government, finance, and industry, and their success created some resentment among Christians. People began to whisper that these converted Christians followed Catholic teachings in public but continued in secret to observe Jewish and Muslim traditions.

A nineteenth-century artist's depiction of Jewish leaders pleading with Ferdinand and Isabella not to exile Spanish Jews

As the Protestant movement got stronger and stronger in the rest of Europe, the whispers against *conversos* became louder and louder. Being truly, purely Christian became a national obsession. It became very important to be able to prove one's "purity of blood." Even if a family had converted hundreds of years before, a person might be passed over for a job because of an "unclean past." Accusations flew. This atmosphere of suspicion added to the power of one of the most feared organizations in history: the Spanish Inquisition.

The Inquisition

Queen Isabella and King Ferdinand wanted to make sure that people were devoted to what they considered the one true faith: Catholicism. Several hundred years before, a pope had organized an international inquisition that had fought and defeated earlier rebels against church teachings. Spain's rulers got permission from the pope to create a uniquely Spanish inquisition. This new inquisition would be run independently by the crown of Spain. Its primary goal would be to unify Spanish faith.

Also called the Holy Office, this religious court sought to identify "false believers": a baptized Jew who still secretly celebrated Jewish holy days such as Passover, a baptized Muslim who secretly fasted during the holy month of Ramadan, a Christian who questioned Catholic teachings—in fact, just about anyone. Everyone was urged to report all the suspicious activities of everyone else. Not just Jews and Muslims, but also Christians could be targeted, simply for celebrating a saint's day differently or reciting a variation on a traditional prayer. Evidence was not necessary: a simple accusation was enough to incur the wrath of the Inquisition. The accused lost their legal rights. As a result, their testimony could be ignored and they could be imprisoned without trial.

Sometimes the Inquisition arrested people for the most minor offenses. One man was detained for smiling when a friend said, "the Virgin Mary." In other cases some Inquisition officials gave in to the temptation of corruption, arresting rich people in order to take their property.

In 1483 Ferdinand appointed a friar named Tomás de Torquemada to be in charge of the Inquisition. Torquemada set up religious courts in fifteen cities and towns across Spain. These courts tried the accused. Meanwhile Inquisition officials inspected travelers entering Spain to make sure they did not carry any Protestant books. The Inquisition searched sailors and sea captains to make sure they did not take Protestant books to colonies in the New World. The Inquisition became Spain's thought police.

Even today the words *Spanish Inquisition* make people think of dark prisons, horrible tortures, and brutal executions. In fact, the penalties for those found guilty were no worse than those used by regular courts of the time. Torture was an accepted

The desire to eliminate heresy did not begin with Ferdinand and Isabella. This painting tells the story of Saint Dominic's burning of heretical books in Spain more than two hundred years before the rulers' time.

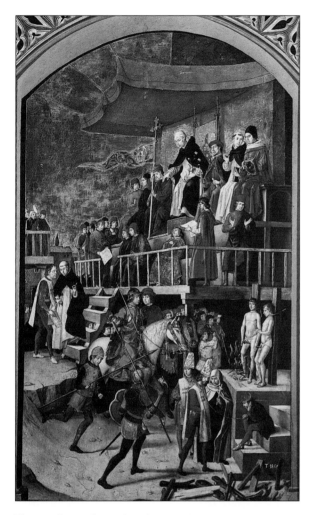

The condemned stand tied to stakes, ready to burn, in this scene of an auto-da-fé.

practice in that day, and the officials of the Spanish Inquisition used it just as kings and princes across Europe did.

In the beginning most punishments were mild, but penalties grew more and more severe as the Inquisition gathered strength. Once a prisoner confessed, or was found guilty, punishments varied widely. Some judged guilty might only be issued a warning or be ordered to attend Mass regularly. They might be fined or relieved of their property. They might be banished from their homes, or whipped with two hundred strokes of a lash. The worst punishment was to be burned alive in a grand public ceremony called an auto-da-fé, or "act of faith."

The Empire as a Holy Mission

The expulsion of non-Christians and the torment inflicted by the Inquisition sound severe today. Yet in the mind of an average sixteenth-century Spaniard, they were completely warranted. There were those who had different ideas, but the majority of faithful Catholics in Spain believed that God had dictated every word of the Bible. They believed that the Son of God had established the Catholic Church and given divine power to the pope. From these two beliefs it was easy for them to conclude that God must have wanted all people to be Christian. As a result, Spaniards came to think that the practices of non-Christians insulted God. An insult to God was a severe crime that demanded strong punishment.

As they traveled around the world, Spanish fleets, governors, traders, explorers, and missionaries carried with them this devotion to the Bible. Every empire needs a reason to justify its right to conquer and subdue weaker nations and peoples. As they came

AN AUTO-DA-FÉ

Every so often Inquisition authorities held an auto-da-fé, an elaborate execution in which heretics were burned alive. It was supposed to strike fear into the hearts of the people, to illustrate the dangers of wrong beliefs, and to strengthen faith.

Early in the morning the bells of the churches tolled solemnly for the souls of those who were about to die. The condemned walked slowly out of prison and took their places in a long procession to the town square. At the head of the procession marched a man holding the flag of the Inquisition. After him came drummers and trumpeters. Then came people carrying a cross, a sword, and an olive branch—symbols of justice and mercy. Armies of priests and monks followed next, each bearing a cross or a banner. Finally came the condemned. Each held a yellow candle and wore a yellow tunic with a large red cross. Sometimes the doomed also wore pointed fools' caps. People lined the streets to watch the parade and shout insults at the condemned.

Eventually all arrived at the square, where a wooden platform had been built. An altar stood in the center of the platform. Near the altar stood the flag and the green cross of the Inquisition.

Then the ceremony began. The audience took an oath to defend the Catholic faith. A priest urged the condemned to repent and told the people to draw a lesson from those about to die. Next he delivered a long sermon. After this the names and crimes of the condemned were read. Since many offenders were executed at one time, this reading could take hours.

The day ended with the executions. The condemned, their hands tied to green crosses, were marched to a place outside of town, followed by the crowd. Executioners tied them to stakes and then burned them alive. The people went home with a searing image of the power of the faith.

to rule one nation after another, the Spanish chose to believe that they were making the world safe for the one true religion: Catholic Christianity.

As the Spanish conquistador killed native peoples and toppled native kings, he thirsted first of all for wealth and power. But he also believed that his conquests served an even greater cause, that of God. He was destroying native societies so that Christian ones could replace them.

Likewise, Spanish missionaries uprooted Indians from their villages and forced them to move to towns built by the Spanish. The missionaries believed that even if they had to be brutal in this world, they were saving the Indians from certain hell in the next world. They believed they were doing Native Americans a favor by making it possible for them to enter God's kingdom in heaven.

At the height of the Spanish empire, halfway through Felipe II's reign, Spanish Christians thought that soon there would be "but one shepherd and one flock in the world" and "one monarch, one empire and one sword." The sword, of course, would be held by the Spanish king. The shepherd would be Christ and the flock would be his Catholic Church. This overwhelming sense of religious righteousness helps to explain why Spain led a holy war against the Turks and Islam. It explains why some Spaniards could approve the burning and torture of nonbelievers. It explains why the Spanish king spent a huge portion of his nation's money fighting wars against Protestants in Germany and the Netherlands.

Religious Art and Architecture

While religion gave Spain a philosophy that justified conquest and repression, faith also inspired Spanish artists to dream and to create. Belief in the one God of three aspects—the Father, the Son, and the Holy Spirit—led to the raising of beautiful cathedrals all over the Spanish countryside. From the outside these Spanish churches looked like massive fortresses for God. Their walls were thick and sometimes rose more than a hundred feet into the air, as if reaching toward heaven. Carvings and decorations—of a distinctly Spanish realism and intensity—were crowded above church doorways and atop domes and spires.

Inside, the churches were cool and dark. The work of the country's most brilliant artists lightened the gloom, often incorporating geometric patterns that harked back to Spain's Islamic heritage. Gems, silver, and gold glittered from a thousand religious objects, satisfying a Spanish taste for elaborate decorations. Masterful paintings adorned the walls. The somber passion of Spanish faith came through in these works. Their vivid colors and their startlingly real images told stories of the Bible that were meant to instill the creed and burn it into the souls of the faithful. Sculptures also adorned the church. Images of the Virgin in stone or wood

IF YOU LIVED IN SPAIN DURING THE AGE OF EXPLORATION

If you had been born in Spain during the Age of Exploration, your way of life would have been determined by the facts of your birth—whether you were a girl or a boy, wealthy or poor, Christian or non-Christian. With this chart you can trace the course your life might have taken as a member of the Christian middle or upper class.

You were born in Madrid. . . .

As a Boy . . .
As a Girl . . .

Within a week of your birth, your family takes you to the local church. There a priest sprinkles water over your head and makes the sign of the cross to baptize you. This ceremony formally admits you to the Catholic Church. Your parents choose a saint who will be your model and protector during your life. They give you the saint's name as your first name.

At about age 7 you learn to read. You study the basic lessons of the church. You receive your first Communion, that is, you eat the bread that Catholics believe is Jesus' body. You start your formal schooling. However, you don't attend school outside your home. Instead instructors come to teach you in your house. You also learn the skills that a soldier needs: knife and sword fighting, horseback riding.

Between ages 14 and 20, if your family can afford it, you go to the university and study for several years. You begin to learn your father's trade or business. You may join the army or the navy. Or you may decide to become a priest. Every family thinks it an honor to give a son to the church. If you do not become a priest, you get married and start a household of your own at about age 20.

As a man you try to be a success at whatever pursuit you have chosen: politics or business or soldiering. You try to have many children, especially sons. In everything you do, you try to uphold the honor of your family. After you get married, you may decide to have mistresses. Although extramarital relations are a crime for women, they are accepted practice for men.

At about age 7 you receive your first Communion. You spend most of your time at home, under the watchful eyes of your parents. You rarely leave the house. You probably go outside only to go to church. You learn to sew and to embroider. You may or may not learn to read; your father may believe that education of women only leads to loose behavior.

Between ages 14 and 20, if you get into trouble, or have male admirers whom your father doesn't like, you may be sent to a convent, where only nuns and other women live. You may also decide on your own that you want to be a nun. Otherwise you get married at about age 20. Your family pays your new husband a dowry of money and household goods.

As a woman your first duty is to give your husband sons. You try to be honorable and to maintain a good reputation. You spend most of your time running your household and rearing your children. To amuse yourself you embroider or perhaps read religious books. Sometimes you might go to the theater, where you sit in the balcony reserved for women. If your husband dies, you have the right to inherit his wealth.

After you die, your children wrap your body in cloth and place it in a coffin. They put a coin in your coffin so that you can pay for passage to heaven. With great lamentation, mourners take your body to the cemetery. For a year after your death your relatives wear black and pray for your soul.

Many of Zurbarán's paintings, such as this one of Saint Peter Nolasco, have a wistful, deeply spiritual quality.

or marble filled sacred buildings. Carved and painted screens rose behind the altar. One screen behind the central altar of Seville's cathedral featured forty-five different religious scenes.

Religious Plays

Religion also provided a forum for playwrights and actors. At most religious festivals, troupes acted out Bible stories in front of an audience. Quevedo, one of the era's most famous playwrights, was known chiefly for his sacred plays, or *auto sacramentales*.

The most elaborate religious plays were held during the festival of Corpus Christi (the name means "body of Christ"), which honored the Eucharist. Each believer who consumed the bread, or Host, during Mass incorporated Christ's body into himself. This belief was central to the Catholic faith. At the festival celebrating Corpus Christi, the Host was carried in procession through the town for all to see. Meanwhile a play entertained the crowds.

A theatrical company hired a writer to compose the play and made elaborate costumes of velvet, satin, and gold and silver cloth. The kingdom's best artists constructed and painted the sets. Wagons, sometimes as many as five, carried the set and the actors. Accompanied by a merry crowd of clowns and dancers, oxen pulled the wagons to a large square. There the actors began the performance. Each actor represented a divine being or concept: God and Satan, Jesus and Mary, faith and heresy. The play made the average person aware of the sacred, cosmic battle in which his or her soul was engaged.

Art served the propaganda of the state: It explained the need for empire and for holy wars, for lavish churches and for the Inquisition. It gave the average person faith that through the grace of the cross, his or her soul could be saved. What was more, the art of the Age of Exploration proclaimed that the fierce soul of Spain could triumph.

SPAIN'S GIFTS TO THE WORLD

CHAPTER FIVE

The influence of Spain's Age of Exploration resounds throughout the modern world. Yet both Spain and its former colonies have mixed feelings about its legacy. Beginning in the eighteenth century, Spain's international influence recovered somewhat after the disasters of the seventeenth century. It still had colonies in Latin America and the Philippines,

but England came to rule the seas and move the world. During the next several centuries, Spain cut itself off from the rest of Europe. France, England, and Germany, in their turns, created world empires and lost them. Meanwhile Spain suffered further losses in a conflict with the United States and a painfully long and bloody civil war. It was not until the 1980s that a democratic government came to power in Spain. This new government opened itself up to the rest of the world. It began to develop Spain's economy. It started to examine Spain's heritage and to confront both the good and the bad. Like most evolving cultures, Spain left a legacy to the world that was a mixture of the exalted and the brutal, the beautiful and the ugly.

New Spain, Old Traditions

Even in this era of space travel, television, and computers, colorful remnants of the golden age live on in Spain. Good manners—an expectation that each person deserves to be treated honorably—are still the norm. The Spanish people still love to dance. The flamenco—a dance developed in southern Spain and incorporating Moorish and Gypsy influences—remains a favorite. Women dressed in frills, satin, and lace clap their hands, stomp, and twirl to the music of guitars. After years of lagging popularity, bullfighting is enjoying a revival. Many people now spend their Sunday afternoons at the bullring, just as Ferdinand and Isabella might have done.

While not all Spaniards today are practicing Catholics, they remain deeply attached to the traditions of the church. Even if they do not attend Mass each Sunday, most Spaniards mark the major events of their lives—birth, marriage, and death—within the Catholic Church. And many maintain a deep religious faith. At the Cathedral of Santiago de Compostela, thousands of pilgrims over the centuries have touched a pillar, leaving the imprint of five fingers. As in imperial days, modern Spaniards flock to Catholic festivals and processions: saint's-day dances,

The modern version of the flamenco was developed during the Age of Exploration. Flamenco dancing is marked by complicated toe and heel clicking and by the fluid arm motions of the dancers.

Spaniards continue to enjoy religious festivals. During Holy Week nightly processions are held in Seville, where participants, hooded and robed, march beside representations of the saints.

evening gatherings. In the spring parades of papier-mâché figures fill the streets of Toledo. The celebration of Corpus Christi still goes on every June. During Holy Week—the week before Easter—businesses close in Seville to celebrate. In that city nightly processions of hooded and robed faithful march behind floats covered with flowers, candles, and bejeweled statues of Mary, Jesus, and the saints. As the floats pass, bands play and bystanders sing. Children call out, *"Guapa! Guapa!"*— "Beautiful! Beautiful!"

The dark side of Spain's religious history has left its mark, however. The effects of ancient intolerance can still be felt, if only slightly. Even today it is not uncommon for a Spaniard to take silent pride in not having Jewish blood.

New Foods for an Old World

Spain can be credited with introducing many New World foods to Europe. When Cortés conquered the Aztecs in Mexico, he developed a taste for chocolate. He brought some back to Spain. When a Spanish princess married a French king, she took chocolate to her new home. From there it spread throughout Europe. Spaniards brought plants from the Americas to Europe: chili peppers, corn, tomatoes, potatoes, and many others.

New Ideas

Spain's discoveries and conquests had an immense impact on European thinking. Spanish descriptions of the Americas as beautiful, simple, and pure inspired European thinkers to write book after book about perfect societies, or utopias, and "noble savages." To many world-weary Europeans, the Native Americans seemed remarkably innocent, kind, and charitable. North and South America seemed to offer an unspoiled land, populated by unspoiled people. Europeans during the Age of Exploration spent little time trying to understand native societies and often underestimated their complexities. As it turned out, life in the Americas differed greatly from the expectations of European thinkers. Injustice, the ruination of landscapes, and war became as common in colonial North and South America as they were in Europe. Even so, the dream inspired many masterpieces of Western literature, such as Sir Thomas More's *Utopia*.

As a result of Spanish conquests, the Catholic faith has become dominant in Latin America. Here a Native American presents a headdress to Pope John Paul II, who was on a visit to the region.

A Model to Follow

Spain also left a political legacy to Europe. Columbus's discovery of the New World jolted other European nations. Jealous of Spain's swift success and new riches, its neighbors rushed to outfit ships of exploration and conquest. Spain's example gave England, France, and the Netherlands a model for building their own empires. Led by Spain, European nations spread Western culture and religion around the world.

Spain was the first European nation to govern such a huge, far-flung empire. No one had ever ruled an empire that literally stretched around the globe. As it tried to do so, imperial Spain had to invent solutions to completely new problems. Many of Madrid's answers are today considered standards in politics and war. Ferdinand of Aragon was the first king to send ambassadors to live permanently in foreign capitals and look out for the interests of the home country. Felipe II established the first international spy organization. Spanish military commanders invented the ranks of general and admiral. Spanish lawyers came up with the notion that the seas should belong to all nations, an idea that is now part of international law.

The challenge of governing subject states in Europe, Africa, the Americas, and Asia also forced Spain to advance technology. In order to correctly represent the first global empire, the Spaniard Alonso de Santa Cruz invented spherical maps. With pirates lurking everywhere, Spanish ship captains could not afford to get lost, so Felipe Guillén perfected the modern compass. The immensity of the silver and gold deposits in Mexico and Peru challenged Spanish engineers to devise new mining methods and new ways to separate precious metals from surrounding rock.

The Spanishness of Spanish Colonies

Of course, Spain's influence was greatest in the countries it conquered and colonized. Spanish language, art, and architecture still have a great impact on these former colonies. The Spanish of Castile is spoken by educated people throughout Latin America. The Spanish preference for ornate decoration and delicate carving is evident in buildings from Cartagena in Colombia to Manila in the Philippines. Colonists and natives built churches in the elaborate style of Spain, incorporating Spanish themes with native ones. The carved screens that stood behind altars in Spain were recreated in the colonies. In Latin America artists combined Spanish religious themes with native patterns and colors. Spanish songs and instruments such as the harp, guitar, and violin resonate throughout Latin American countries. Dances in those countries also incorporate elements from the Iberian Peninsula.

The small details of Spanish life were likewise transmitted to the

This cathedral in Bolivia has lavish, complex decorations that hark back to the ornate interiors of churches in Spain.

colonies. Even today most houses in Latin America are roofed with Spanish-style red tiles. Many Latin American towns are laid out in the grid pattern that became popular during the Age of Exploration. Nicaraguan and Argentinian peasants alike use a Mediterranean-style scratch plow to prepare the soil for planting. Indians in the Andes use a Spanish-style net to catch fish.

Along with these material contributions, Spanish cultural ideas seeped into the spirit of the colonists. Spaniards, in imperial times and now, placed a great importance on honor and respect, home and family. Long after the end of the colonial era these ideas continue to wield real power in Latin America and the Philippines. In those countries some people will still fight over a point of honor and to uphold their good name. Individuals tend to place the needs of their families before their own desires. In many former colonies it's not unusual for grandparents, parents, and children to share the same house.

The Church

Perhaps Spain's most profound legacy to the New World and the Philippines is the Catholic faith. Before they were conquered, many native societies had a deep sense of the divine. When their temples were torn down and they were subjugated, they understandably longed for comfort and protection. The mystery and hope of the Catholic faith appealed to many native peoples.

Like the Spaniards, the new Christians became devoted to the Virgin Mary and the saints. They celebrated religious days with Spanish-style processions and festivals. Today Catholic baptisms, marriages, and death rites are a fixture of life in Latin America and the Philippines.

Political Problems

Spain in the Age of Exploration achieved great glory and wealth. However, it also saw sharp conflicts between rich and poor. It emphasized status and nobility rather than industry and business sense. It tended to resist change. It relied on force—war—to impose its will on others. At one time or another these characteristics could also have described the circumstances of the Spanish colonies.

As in the home country, the economies of the colonies stressed investment in land and livestock. People thought it was more honorable to stay home and collect rents than to toil in business and industry. Colonial upper classes spent most of their energy trying to recreate the grandeur of the Spanish nobility. They spent much of their time and money on elaborate houses, expensive clothes, and armies of servants. At the same time, the work of building new nations and strong economies was sometimes neglected. As a result, Latin America and the Philippines were slow to develop the industry and the commerce that control the modern world. They had to borrow money from other countries. Today almost all of Spain's former colonies struggle because they owe impossibly large amounts to foreign banks.

A country in which there are two rigid classes—one very rich and the other very poor—is unstable. People who are starving and unhappy eventually try to take what society does not give them. As a consequence the Philippines and Latin America have often had to deal with rebellions. Although much has changed in the former colonies, at least part of the responsibility for these problems rests on the shoulders of Spain's imperial rulers. It should be remembered, however, that other European colonial empires did not do much better. Former French and English colonies of Africa struggle with very similar challenges.

The Legacy of the Spanish Spirit

Despite these problems, Spain's Age of Exploration has given the world much to celebrate. The literature of that period still enriches the world. Students in high schools and colleges today read Cervantes' novel, *Don Quixote*. Modern drama owes a debt to the Spanish play *La Celestina*. Broadway musicals and Hollywood movies in part trace their beginnings to the rowdy theaters of sixteenth-century Spain.

And, of course, the artists of Spain's golden age continue to delight.

THE PRADO

The kings of Spain had a passion for pictures. Luckily for modern eyes, the collections of these monarchs have been gathered into a museum. Called the Prado, the museum was built in 1785.

From the reign of Carlos V until the reign of Felipe IV, Spain's monarchs put together one of the finest art collections ever amassed. The haunting faces of Velázquez's portraits are there as well as the brilliant, deep colors of Zurbarán's religious pictures, and the stretched-out spooky figures of El Greco's paintings. Other famous European artists have been included in the collection. The museum owns about four thousand paintings and displays five hundred at a time. It keeps the extra paintings in storage or lends them to other museums.

The Prado's collections reflect royal tastes and do not represent a complete history of Western art. For instance, Spanish kings didn't buy the works of painters from England and France, Spain's political rivals. For this reason some art critics say the Prado can't be called the world's greatest museum. Supporters, however, counter that the quality of all the pictures may make it the most exhilarating museum in the world.

The somber colors of Velázquez, the rich fabrics of Zurbarán, the young faces of Murillo, the bizarre visions of El Greco—all continue to draw art lovers around the world.

Centuries later, the pride and beauty, the power and faith, the tradition and invention of Spain's Age of Exploration continue to influence and inspire the modern world.

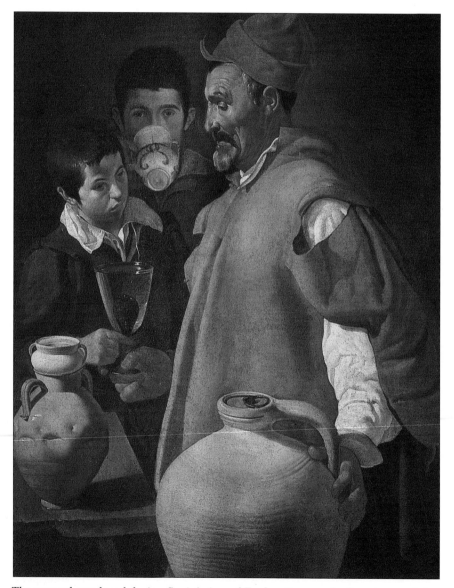

The artwork produced during Spain's Age of Exploration can be found around the world today. This Velázquez painting, The Waterseller of Seville, *hangs in Apsley House, London.*

Spain in the Age of Exploration: A Chronology

1469   Isabella of Castile marries Ferdinand of Aragon

1474   Isabella and Ferdinand are crowned queen and king of Castile and León

1479   Ferdinand ascends the throne of Aragon

1481   The Inquisition begins

1492   Granada surrenders, ending the Reconquest of Christian Spain; Spain's Jews are expelled; Columbus lands in America

1502   Spain's Moors are expelled

1504   Isabella dies

1512   Ferdinand conquers Navarre

1516   Ferdinand dies

1517   Charles V (Carlos I) becomes king of Spain, eventually to wear "seventeen crowns"

1521   Hernán Cortés conquers the Aztecs of Mexico

1535   Conquest of Inca empire in South America

1555   Felipe II becomes king

1560   Felipe II makes Madrid the capital of Spain

1571   A fleet led by Spain defeats the Turks at Lepanto

1580   Felipe II gains the throne of Portugal

1588   The Armada is destroyed

1598   Felipe III becomes king

1609   The Moriscos (converted Muslims) are expelled from Spain

1621   Felipe IV becomes king

1640   Portugal regains its independence

1648   The Netherlands wins independence from Spain

1665   Carlos II becomes king

1700   Carlos II dies; Spain's role as a world power ends

GLOSSARY

armada: a fleet of warships

auto-da-fé: public ceremony announcing the sentences imposed on those found guilty by the Inquisition

auto sacramentale: a religious play

baptism: a ceremony that marks the beginning of Christian life

Catholic: literally means "universal." The primary Christian church during the Age of Exploration

comedia: a dramatic play

Communion: the part of the Catholic Mass during which people eat bread and wine that they believe to be Christ's body and blood

confirmation: a religious ceremony by which one becomes a full member of the church

conquistadores: Spanish conquerors in the New World

Corpus Christi: literally, the "body of Christ." A festival honoring the bread or Host that Catholics believe is Christ's body

dialect: a regional variety of a language

Eucharist: a sacrament and the central act of worship in the Catholic Church, in which bread and wine are consumed in remembrance of Jesus Christ

fast: to go without food. A common Christian penance

heresy: an opinion or practice that differs from established religious teachings

heretic: a person who commits heresy

hidalgo: a low-ranking Spanish noble, equivalent to an English knight

honor: a code of behavior that stresses respect, glory, honesty, pride, dignity

horizon: the line where the earth and the sky meet

Inquisition: a court in the Catholic Church that tried to suppress and punish heresy

martyr: one who suffers death rather than surrender religious principles

masquerade: a party or parade in which people wear masks or costumes

Mass: a Catholic church service

matador: a bullfighter

miracle: an event that cannot be explained and is judged to be a result of divine intervention

peninsula: a piece of land surrounded on three sides by water

pilgrim: a religious person who travels to a sacred place

pilgrimage: the journey of a pilgrim

For Further Reading

Anderson, David. *The Spanish Armada*. New York: Hampstead Press, 1988.

Brenner, Barbara. *If You Were There in 1492*. New York: Bradbury, 1991.

Columbus, Christopher. *I, Columbus: My Journal 1492–3*. New York: Walker, 1990.

Don Quixote: Tales of La Mancha. Family Home Entertainment. Ziv International, 1982. Videocassette.

Helly, Mathilde, and Rémi, Courgeon. *Montezuma and the Aztecs*. New York: Henry Holt, 1996.

Hodges, Margaret. *Don Quixote and Sancho Panza*. Adapted from *Don Quixote of La Mancha* by Miguel de Cervantes Saavedra. New York: Scribner, 1992.

Lincoln, Margarette. *The Pirate's Handbook*. New York: Cobblehill/Dutton, 1995.

Marrin, Albert. *The Sea King: Sir Francis Drake and His Times*. New York: Atheneum, 1995.

Meltzer, Milton. *Columbus and the World Around Him*. New York: Franklin Watts, 1990.

Pettenuzzo, Brenda. *I Am a Roman Catholic*. New York: Franklin Watts, 1985.

Schubert, Adrian. *The Land and People of Spain*. New York: HarperCollins, 1992.

Sinnot, Susan. *Extraordinary Hispanic Americans*. Chicago: Childrens Press, 1991.

Stevens, Paul. *Ferdinand and Isabella*. New York: Chelsea House, 1988.

Stierlin, Henri. *The Cultural History of Spain*. London: Aurum Press, 1984.

Where Do You Think You're Going, Christopher Columbus? Weston, Connecticut: Weston Woods, 1991. Videocassette, 35 min.

BIBLIOGRAPHY

Adzigian, Joy, and A. Hoyt Hobbs. *Fielding's Spain 1995*. Redondo Beach, California: Fielding Worldwide, 1995.

Boorstin, Daniel J. *The Discoverers*. New York: Random House, 1983.

Defourneux, Marcelin. *Daily Life in Spain in the Golden Ages*. Translated by Newton Branch, London: George Allen and Unwin, 1970.

Elliott, J.H. *Imperial Spain 1469–1716*. New York: St. Martin's Press, 1964.

Elliott, J.H. *Spain and Its World 1500–1700: Selected Essays*. New Haven: Yale University Press, 1989.

Ellis, Havelock. *The Soul of Spain*. Toronto: Macmillan, 1937.

Fuentes, Carlos. *The Buried Mirror: Reflections on Spain and the New World*. New York: Houghton Mifflin, 1992.

Haliczer, Stephen, ed. and trans. *Inquisition and Society in Early Modern Europe*. Totowa, New Jersey: Barnes & Noble, 1987.

Highfield, Roger, ed. *Spain in the Fifteenth Century 1369–1516*. London: Macmillan, 1972.

Kamen, Henry. *Golden Age Spain*. Atlantic Highlands, New Jersey: Humanities Press International, 1988.

Kamen, Henry. *Inquisition and Society in Spain in the Sixteenth and Seventeenth Centuries*. Bloomington: Indiana University Press, 1985.

Kamen, Henry. *Spain 1469–1714: A Society of Conflict*. London and New York: Longman, 1983.

Lynch, John. *Spain Under the Habsburgs*. Vol. 2. New York: New York University Press, 1981.

Mariéjol, Jean Hippolyte. Translated and edited by Benjamin Keen. *The Spain of Ferdinand and Isabella*. New Brunswick, New Jersey: Rutgers University Press, 1961.

McAlister, Lyle N. *Spain and Portugal in the New World 1492–1700*. Minneapolis: University of Minnesota Press, 1984.

Parry, J.H. *The Spanish Seaborne Empire*. New York: Knopf, 1966.

Salmon, Edward Dwight. *Imperial Spain: The Rise of the Empire and the Dawn of Modern Sea-Power*. Westport, Connecticut: Greenwood Press, 1971.

Sugden, John. *Sir Francis Drake*. New York: Henry Holt, 1990.

INDEX

Page numbers for illustrations are in boldface.

ABOUT THE AUTHOR

Heather Millar grew up in San Francisco, a city founded by Spanish conquistadores and priests. She attended Stanford University, where she studied history and Chinese. After graduating from college she spent eighteen months living in China. While living overseas she also worked for the *London Daily Telegraph* and traveled throughout Asia. She writes about history and current affairs for publications such as the *New York Times*, *Business Week*, and the *Atlantic Monthly*.

Ms. Millar lives in Manhattan with her husband, Peter, a newspaper editor, and her stepdaughter, Maureen.